21世纪高等院校·影视艺术经典教材
FILM & TELEVISION ART

电影经典文本导读
Guide to Classic Film Texts

宋雁蓉　主编
施嘉敏 朱琳　副主编

中国国际广播出版社

本书系北京电影学院研究项目“科技创新服务能力建设－高精尖学科建设－电影学”（项目编号：PXM2019-014220-000096）研究成果。

编者语

《电影经典文本导读》是一本电影原文文本教材，可供有一定英语语言基础和电影基础的高校本科生或研究生使用。

本书涵盖了电影史上的重要时刻、重要导演及其创作理念、重要电影理论、经典影片分析，既有学术性又有可读性和实用性，在帮助学生拓展专业知识，提升学术能力和观影体验的同时，也能在具体的拍摄实践中发挥启迪性作用。

在进行了广泛深入的调研、论证，精心的资料搜集和设计，并对部分材料进行了试用后，我和我的团队认真编写完成了这本《电影经典文本导读》教材。

本书共分 10 个单元，每个单元有 A 和 B 两个阅读语篇。阅读 A 是关于影史上的重要时刻、重要导演及其创作理念等内容。阅读 B 是相关的影片分析内容。列出的单词和词组是为了让学生把更多的时间和精力转向对原文文本的关注，加强对文本整体意识的把握和欣赏文本的流畅性。思考题能训练学生的分析、归纳能力。选词填空能加强学生对专业词汇和电影专业知识的掌握及灵活运用。英汉互译是通过翻译训练加强学生对语篇的理解。根据上下文猜测词义能够培养学生把电影专业词汇和词汇的语境紧密联系起来。

阅读外国语言文本的目的无非是要加强和提高听、说、读、写、译的能力，并在此基础上理解、欣赏或批评域外文化，进而开展跨文化交际，这当中涵盖技能层面和文化层面。希望本书的出版能够在理解、欣赏和批判作者观点和原文文本内容的前提下，激发学生学术研究和艺术创作的灵感。

感谢编写组成员的辛勤工作，感谢所有关心支持我们编写工作的老师和同学们。

编者

2019 年 12 月 26 日

CONTENTS

Unit Three

Unit Four

Unit Five

Unit One

Text A

The Birth of Film

para 1 Three things were essential to developing projected motion pictures as we know them today: a camera with a sufficiently high shutter speed to freeze motion, a filmstrip capable of taking multiple exposures swiftly, and a means of projecting the developed images on a screen. The race to achieve that goal reached fever pitch in the 1890s, and the first to cross the finish line was France.

para 2 On March 22,1895, the brothers Auguste and Louis Lumière gave a historic public showing of projected film at the Society for Encouraging National Industry. Louis Lumière showed a number of slides, some of them colored. But the small audience was more interested in the brothers' short film, called *Workers Leaving the Lumière Factory*. The wonder-filled audience demanded that the film, which depicted workers leaving the Lumières' Lyons factory at dinnertime, consisting of some eight hundred photographs and lasting one minute, be shown again.

para 3 One month later, on April 21, the first projected movie shown publicly in America was screened in New York City. Using a device originally called the Panoptikon and subsequently the Eidoloscope—the names of many of these early devices seem straight out of science fiction—the brothers Otway and Gray Latham showed a film to guests and reporters at their workshop on Frankfort Street. According to the New York Sun, it "portrayed the antics of some boys at play in a park. They wrestled, jumped, fought, and tumbled over one another. Near where the boys were romping a man sat reading a paper and smoking a pipe. Even the puffs of smoke could be plainly seen".

para 4 Thomas Edison, who had developed the Kinetoscope, a movie peep show for individuals, was furious and threatened a lawsuit. It would not be until a year later, on April 23,1896, that "the wizard of Menlo Park" would publicly present projected films, which he did by using the Vitascope projector at Koster and Bial's Music Hall at Thrity-fourth Street and Broadway. Macy's department store is located there now, and the event is memorialized with a plaque.

para 5 On May 20,1895, the Lathams beat both Edison and the French when they opened a public exhibition space, at 156 Broadway, where for a few pennies, patrons could watch movies. And what could one see? According to a newspaper account: "You'll sit comfortably and see fighters hammering each other, circuses, suicides, hangings, electrocutions, shipwrecks… Almost anything, in fact, in which there is action, just as if you were on the spot during the actual events."

para 6 So if the French were the first to project films publicly, the Americans were the first to create a business to make money from it. Still, from a broader historical view, these accomplishments seem like the equivalent of a photo finish. The elements that could make cinema a reality were falling into place, and many cinematic alchemists were turning them to gold. The Lumières, as it turned out, were not even the first in Europe to project films for a paying audience. The German Max Skladanowsky, who invented a motion-picture camera and a projector, which he called the Bioskope, inched them out with a film showing at the Berlin Wintergarten, on November 1, 1895.

para 7 Something was certainly in the air. The turn of the century was a period of tremendous technological development, firing imaginations with visions of speed. Marconi invented wireless telegraphy in 1895, and the Wright brothers would take flight in 1903—it's no wonder that even pictures had to move. And it's hardly surprising that early cinema was obsessed with trains and cars, powerful imagery of acceleration.

para 8 Still, in the run-up to film projection, no one really seems to have had a sense of the immensity of what was being created—the seventh art form, which would in many ways change the world. In part that was because film projection came about incrementally and would never have been possible without the multiple breakthroughs that preceded it. One such milestone was certainly when Edison first publicly demonstrated the popular and profitable Kinetoscope, which permitted individuals to watch moving pictures through a peephole in 1891. But before Edison and his younger colleague, William Kennedy-Laurie Dickson, a photographer and inventor who led the team that developed the Kinetoscope, came many others.

para 9 Among them was the English photographer Eadweard Muybridge, who in the 1870s developed series photography showing animals in motion, using multiple cameras. In 1882, in France, French physiologist Etienne-Jules Marey, using a camera shaped like a rifle called the Chronophotographic Gun, shot the first series of photos taken by a single camera in order to study the motion of birds and bats in flight.

para 10 One could go back further, to the early developments in photography. In 1839, Louis-Jacques-Mandé Daguerre developed the photographic process of the daguerreotype. An Englishman, William Henry Fox Talbot, demonstrated a negative photographic process that allowed multiple reproductions from a negative. Obviously, without photography, there would be no cinema.

para 11 The idea of projecting images goes back to the seventeenth century: in 1646, Athanasius Kircher published the first description of the magic lantern in print, in Ars Magna Lucis et Umbrae. Using concave glass, the magic lantern was the first apparatus capable of projecting images and was widely used in Europe. In 1665, Samuel Pepys wrote about one in his diary: "Comes by agreement Mr. Reeves bringing me a lanthorn, with pictures in glass, to make strange things on a wall, very pretty."

para 12 Perhaps a good place to start, however , is with the basic principle that makes moving pictures possible, called the persistence of vision, which was first described in an 1824 paper by the English polymath Peter Mark Roget. Roget was primarily interested in medicine, but he is best known for his thesaurus, which was first printed in 1852 and has never since been out of print. Because the brain retains images cast on the retina for a fraction of a second after they disappear, Roget asserted that viewing sixteen images per second conveys the impression of motion. While he didn't pursue the notion, he inspired a number of inventors who created toy-like machines that produced the illusion of motion. In 1832, the Phenakistoscope, invented simultaneously by the Belgian Joseph Plateau and the Austrain Simon von Stampfer, created motion pictures with phased drawings presented on a revolving disk. Two years later, William George Horner developed the zoetrope, which presented images with a rotating drum.

para 13 There would be no cinema, however, until photographic processes were sufficiently advanced. The art of photography—portraits, landscapes, cityscapes—improved steadily in the second half of the century, and those improvements came from scientists and artists.

Screen for Reference

La Sortie des usines Lumière（《工厂大门》，1895 年，短片）
A Trip to the Moon（《月球旅行记》，1902 年，短片）
The Great Train Robbery（《火车大劫案》，1903 年，短片）
Afgrunden（《无底洞》，1910 年，短片）

New Words

filmstrip /'fɪlmˌstrɪp/ *n.*
a series of transparencies in a strip for projection 电影胶片
antic /'æntɪk/ *adj.*
ludicrously eccentric 古怪的，滑稽可笑的
wrestle /'resl/ *v.*
take part in a fight, either as sport or in earnest 摔跤，斗争，斟酌
tumble /'tʌmbl/ *v.*
fall down, as if collapsing 摔倒，倒塌，滚动，打滚
plaque /plæk/ *n.*
an ornamental tablet, typically of metal, porcelain, or wood fixed to a wall or other surface in commemoration of a person or event 纪念牌匾，纪念牌
patron /'peɪtrən/ *n.*
a person who gives financial or other support to a person, organization, or cause 企业主，雇主，老板，掌柜
shipwreck /'ʃɪprek/ *n.*
the destruction of a ship at sea by sinking or breaking up 海难，遇难船
equivalent /ɪ'kwɪvələnt/ *adj.*
equal in value, amount, function, meaning, etc. 等价的，相等的，同意义的
wireless /'waɪərləs/ *adj.*
using radio, microwaves, etc. to transmit signals 无线的，无线电的

acceleration /əkˌseləˈreɪʃn/ *n.*

a vehicle's capacity to gain speed 加速，促进

immensity /ɪˈmensəti/ *n.*

the extremely large size, scale, or extent of something 巨大，无限，广大

daguerreotype /dəˈɡerətaɪp/ *n.*

an early photographic process 达盖尔银版照片

concave /kɔnˈkeɪv/ *adj.*

curved inward like the inner surface of a bowl or sphere 凹的，凹面的

Phrase and Expression

be obsessed with

be addicted to or be crazy about 沉迷于，痴迷于，迷恋

come about

happen; change direction 发生，产生；改变方向

I. Reading Comprehension.

1.What three things were essential to developing projected motion pictures?

2.What does the "goal" (Line 5, Para. 1) refer to?

3.What the clip in the film that audience demanded was shown again?

4.Who showed the first projected movie to public in New York City?

5.If you were at 156 Broadway on May 20,1895, what would you be seeing?

6.Who invented a motion-picture camera and a projector?

7.What did Thomas Edison do as a milestone in the history of cinema?

8.Why does the author say "without photography, there would be no cinema"?

II. Fill in the Blanks with the Words Given Below.

As feature films became standardized, Hollywood filmmaker established firmer guidelines for creating intelligible plot. These guidelines have changed ( ) since then. Hollywood plots consist of clear ( ) of causes and effects, and most of these involve character psychology. Each major character is given a set of comprehensible, ( ) traits. Hollywood protagonist is typically ( ), trying to achieve success in work, sports, or some other activity. The hero's goal conflicts with the desires of ( ) characters, creating a struggle that is resolved only at the end. Hollywood films usually ( ) interest by presenting two interdependent plot lines. Almost inevitably one of these involves ( ). The plot also arouses ( ) through deadlines, escalating conflicts, and last-minute ( ). These principles of storytelling have contributed to the ( ) international success of American films.

a. public-oriented b. enduring c. little d. chains e. other f. choppy g. goal-oriented h. consistent i. suspense j. rescues k. romance l. intensify

III. Translation.

Section A: Put the followings into Chinese.

1. The wonder-filled audience demanded that the film, which depicted workers leaving the Lumière' Lyons factory at dinnertime, consisting of some eight hundred photographs and lasting one minute, be shown again.

2. Still, from a broader historical view, these accomplishments seem like the equivalent of a photo finish. The elements that could make cinema a reality were falling into place, and many cinematic alchemists were turning them to gold.

3. Something was certainly in the air. The turn of the century was a period of tremendous technological development, firing imagination with

visions of speed.

4. In the run-up to film projection, no one really seems to have had a sense of the immensity of what was being created—the seventh art form, which would in many ways change the world.

5. Because the brain retains images cast on the retina for a fraction of a second after they disappear, Roget asserted that viewing sixteen images per second conveys the impression of motion. While he didn't pursue the notion, he inspired a number of inventors who created toy-like machines that produced the illusion of motion.

Section B: Put the followings into English.

爱森斯坦利用肢体与情感的冲突驱动行动。表演者的表演与人物的塑造并非依照传统的约定俗成去建立、发展，而是利用各种体态和能够迅速波及故事动态情感层面的综合反应来演绎。

____

____

____

____

____

Text B

Still 1-1

Still 1-2

The Battleship Potemkin

para 1 The cinematic term montage is erroneously generalized and used all too freely to indicate rapid-paced editing, or it is tossed around encased in the more nebulous phrase "MTV editing". The most significant definition of montage concerns the theories and practice of early Russian filmmakers including Sergei Eisenstein, Vsevolod Pudovkin, Alexander Dovzhenko and Lev Kuleshov.

para 2 Films at the dawn of the cinema were composed of a single shot. The pioneering Lumière brothers set up their camera and recorded an event such as *Workers Leaving the Lumière Factory* or *The Arrival of the Mail Train*. Eventually, filmmakers began to experiment with shot-by-shot visual storytelling. Among those responsible for this development are Edwin S. Porter with *The Great Train Robbery* and D.W. Griffith, whose work led to the creation of a cinematic language that utilized angles, shot size, composition, and a number of other elements to forge a story during the editorial process. Working with these principles, the Russians created a powerful visual grammar that employed the graphic dynamics of each shot which they edited into montages.

para 3 Sergei Eisenstein was the most consequential filmmaker of this movement. His achievements on *The Battleship Potemkin, October*, and *Strike*, along with dense intellectual writings on his theory of montage published as the books *Film Form and Film Sense*, created the basis for Russian montage. The subject as practiced by Eisenstein is complex. The presiding concept was the result of a collision effect between shots, each designed for their graphic, narrative, social, and optimum political purpose. Classical Hollywood editing was based on continuity and the matching of shots to link images seamlessly.

para 4 *The Battleship Potemkin* (1925) is the central work for understanding the power and aesthetic methods of the Russian school of montage. The dramatic structure is partitioned into five parts. Part One, "The Men and the Maggots", deals with a revolt by the sailors of the battleship Potemkin against the brutal captain and his officers. When the men are forced to eat meat rotten with maggots, a breakdown in social order occurs. Crashing waves on the shore poetically signal turbulence on the ship. A sailor wakes up the sleeping crew and begins to rouse them with passions of revolt. The sailors lying in hammocks are lit in a lazy but oppressive light. As the man speaks, a flurry of reaction shots signal the building anger.

para 5 Throughout *The Battleship Potemkin* the montage pace modulates according to the emotional content or the action, an important principle often ignored by current practitioners of the style. This is not fast editing purely for the sake of quick pace to keep the drama moving, but is carefully designed visual storytelling orchestrated to unfold a narrative in a kinetic, didactic, and ultimately visceral manner.

para 6 *The Battleship Potemkin* remains a twentieth century canonical work because it contains and demonstrates the properties of shot design and shot-by-shot storytelling driven by the editing process. It is the prehistory of much of what we call cinema. Eisenstein's daring experiment invented the very building blocks of cinematic grammar and defined editing, the medium's one original art and craft, as the key to dynamic visual story-telling.

I. Context Clues.

Guess the meanings of the following with the help of the context clues.

1. nebulous phrase ______________
2. shot-by-shot visual storytelling ______________
3. graphic dynamics ______________
4. consequential ______________
5. Russian school of montage ______________

II. Questions for Consideration.

1. Can you, according to your film knowledge you learned, list some masterpieces of the three filmmakers—Vsevolod Pudovkin, Alexander Dovzhenko and Lev Kuleshov?

2. What the properties does *The Battleship Potemkin* contain and demonstrate?

Unit Two

Text A

MGM and Its Stars

para 1 Stars were the prize commodity at Loew's/MGM, although directors and writers were highly valued as well. These were employees whose talents could not be easily defined and cultivated, who could not be trained and regulated like other craftsmen and technicians. But as important as they were to feature filmmaking, they had precious little control over their individual careers or their pictures. At MGM, it was Louis Mayer who controlled their careers, at least where contracts and principal casting were concerned. There were rare occasions when Schenck or Loew cut a deal, but for the most part Mayer negotiated with and signed the studio's star performers, directors, and writers, thus supplying the key resources for Thalberg's production operations. Mayer was a consummate tactician and psychologist, well known for his ability to cultivate and control MGM's top talent, especially its stars. He was aware that he could not shape an actor's personality or foist just any player on the audience. "The public makes the stars", Mayer was fond of saying—and this attitude was a complement to Thalberg's reliance on public previews to test-market MGM's pictures. But while Mayer and Thalberg relied on audience feedback to confirm their judgments, both were adamant about the judgments being their own. Success necessarily bred confidence, and with MGM's prosperity their dual control over the production process steadily tightened.

para 2 That control was challenged, of course, since stars tended to have powerful egos and were well aware of their box-office clout. Mayer in fact had rather significant battles in 1927-1928 with two top stars, Greta Garbo and Lillian Gish, and each of those skirmishes was revealing of the star's authority at MGM and of the complex interplay of star persona and studio style. A few weeks after MGM secured Gilbert's stardom in *The Big Parade*, the studio released *The Torrent*, a routine melodrama featuring one Greta Gustafsson, whom Mayer had discovered a year earlier whilc scouting talent in Germany. She changed her name to Garbo, and in *The Torrent* she displayed that rare combination of beauty, personality, and dramatic ability that was the essence of stardom. Garbo's breakthrough came in late 1926 when she was teamed with Gilbert for *Flesh and the Devil,* and when that picture hit, she demanded that her $600-per-week salary be adjusted to reflect her market value. Mayer refused and Garbo bolted—all the way to her native Sweden, in fact, where she remained for seven months until Mayer and company came around to her demand of $5,000 a week. Mayer caved in not only because of Garbo's market value and star appeal, but also because her screen persona was so well suited to MGM's prestige strategy and emerging high-gloss style which favored romantic melodrama and light comedy set in a contemporary milieu populated by glamorous, sophisticated characters.

para 3 Lillian Gish provided an interesting counterpoint to Garbo.

She came to the studio an established star, but one whose personality was distinctly at odds with MGM's style and whose degree of control over the production process—by way of script approval, granted by Schenck when he signed her—put her at odds with Mayer and Thalberg's system. Gish delivered strong performances in *The Scarlet Letter* (1926) and *The Wind* (1928), two brooding dramas directed by Victor Seastrom which Thalberg appreciated for their critical prestige, but which Mayer found utterly distasteful. Mayer was so displeased with the downbeat finale of *The Wind*, in which Gish descends into madness and awaits certain death after killing a man who had molested her, that he demanded a more favorable outcome for the virtuous heroine. As he had with Tess, Mayer sent the picture back into production for a revised ending. Gish protested bitterly, as did Seastrom, but Mayer stood firm—and without protest from Thalberg, who had personally supervised the production. *The Wind* was the last picture Gish or Seastrom did for MGM, and their departure was as inevitable as Mayer's buckling under to Garbo's salary demand. Gish's penchant for grim realism and "serious" drama had no place at MGM, where quality and style were a function of polish, poise, and glamour—qualities personified by Garbo, who would never work for any other studio but MGM.

para 4 Louis Mayer kept the stars in line and under contract, and Irving Thalberg kept them busy. They relied on a number of key executives for assistance, none of whom had any real visibility outside the studio. Mayer's right-hand man where the plant itself was concerned was E. J. "Eddie" Mannix. Ironically enough, Mannix first came to Culver City as a confederate of Nick Schenck, who sent him out West in late

1925 to keep an eye on Mayer and Thalberg after their new contracts guaranteed them a bigger portion of Loew's/MGM profits. There may have been an intimidation factor involved, since Mannix gave the impression of being something of a thug. Decades earlier, when Nick Schenck and his brother Joe were still in the amusement park business, Eddie Mannix had been a bouncer at one of their parks. The Schencks soon learned that Mannix had a mind for business and a knack for diplomacy in labor-management relations, so he wound up in the front office. Once he got used to California, Mannix found he liked Hollywood and that he had much in common with Louis Mayer. Before long he was a fast friend of the MGM boss, and under Mayer's guidance he learned the movie business and sharpened his management skills. Within a year of his arrival Mannix was managing the studio at executive rank and even supervising an occasional feature.

para 5 So Mayer managed the human resources and Mannix the facilities, and both worked closely with Thalberg to plan the overall production program. This required meticulous scheduling and script development, close collaboration with the various department heads to ensure efficiency and to maintain production values, and careful supervision of each picture. Thalberg relied on a coterie of close associates to facilitate actual production. There were five key "Thalberg men": Harry Rapf, Bernie Hyman, Hunt Stromberg, Al Lewin, and Paul Bern. Others came and went, of course, but these men worked closest and longest—with Thalberg once his system stabilized. Generally referred to as supervisors, the five were forerunners of the Hollywood line producer. They worked closely with Thalberg to prepare projects for production, and then they monitored shooting, keeping an eye on budget and schedule as well as the day-to-day activities on the set.

Each of them was handpicked by Thalberg, and each was fairly unique in terms of training and talent. Bernie Hyman was similar to Thalberg in personality and upbringing—a New York street kid with a public school education who was introverted and somewhat cerebral, but with a sense of humor and a quick wit. At MGM, Hyman tended to supervise the middle- and low-budget pictures. He shared those duties with Harry Rapf, who came to movies via vaudeville and carnival shows. His tastes were cruder and his judgement more pragmatic than those of his colleagues, but Rapf was a highly efficient and capable supervisor. The other three Thalberg men came up through the writers' ranks. Hunt Stromberg started as a reporter in the Midwest, came to the Coast to work as a publicist, and then became an independent producer before joining MGM in 1925. Both Paul Bern and Al Lewin had solid academic credentials, Bern from the American Academy of Dramatic Arts and Lewin from New York University and Harvard. Both started at MGM as screenwriters and became head of the scenario department before graduating to supervisor status.

Screen for Reference

The Wind（《风》，1928 年，米高梅制作，丽莲·吉许主演）

Queen Christina（《瑞典女王》，1933 年，米高梅制作，葛丽泰·嘉宝主演）

Fury（《怒火》，1936 年，米高梅制作，西尔维娅·西德尼主演）

Waterloo Bridge（《魂断蓝桥》，1940 年，米高梅制作，费雯·丽主演）

Gaslight（《煤气灯下》，1944 年，米高梅制作，英格丽·褒曼主演）

New Words

consummate /kən'sʌmət/ *adj.*

make (a marriage or relationship) complete by having sexual intercourse 至上的，

完美的，圆满的

tactician /tæk'tɪʃn/ *n.*

a person who uses a carefully planned strategy to achieve a specific end 战术家，谋士

adamant /'ædəmənt/ *adj.*

firmly or stubbornly determined; unwilling to be persuade 坚决的，坚强的，倔强的，坚定不移的

skirmish /'skɜːmɪʃ/ *n.*

an episode of irregular or unpremeditated fighting, especially between small or outlying parts of armies or fleets 小冲突，小规模战斗，小争论

melodrama /'melədrɑːmə/ *n.*

a sensational dramatic piece with exaggerated characters and exciting events intended to appeal to the emotions 闹剧，情节剧，音乐剧

milieu /miː'ljɜː/ *n.*

a person's social environment 环境，周围，出身背景

sophisticated /sə'fɪstɪˌkeɪtɪd/ *adj.*

having, revealing, or involving a great deal of worldly experience and knowledge of fashion and culture 复杂的，精致的；久经世故的，富有经验的

counterpoint /'kaʊntərpɔɪnt/ *n.*

the technique of setting, writing, or playing a melody or melodies in conjunction with another, according to fixed rules. A thing that forms a pleasing or notable contrast to something else 复调，对位法，旋律配合；对应物

heroine /'heroʊɪn/ *n.*

a woman admired for her courage, outstanding achievements, or noble qualities 女主角，女英雄，女杰出人物

confederate /kən'fedərət/ *n.*

one of a group of people, states, or political parties who have united for a particular purpose, especially a political one 同盟国，同盟者

knack /næk/ *n.*

skill at performing some special task; ability 诀窍，熟练技术，本领

meticulous /mə'tɪkjələs/ *adj.*

showing great attention to detail; very careful and precise 一丝不苟的，小心翼翼的，拘泥小节的

forerunner /'fɔːrʌnər/ *n.*

a person or thing that precedes the coming or development of someone or something else 先驱，先驱者；预兆

Phrase and Expression

reliance on

dependence on 依靠，信赖

the essence of

most important or indispensable quality of something 精髓

at odds with

be disagreeing or quarrelling with somebody about something 与……争执，意见不一致

I. Reading Comprehension.

1. What was Louis Mayer known for?
2. What was one of reasons for MGM's prosperity?
3. What constituted a challenge to Mayer's power?
4. How did the author evaluate Greta Gustafsson?
5. Why did Mayer meet Garbo's demands?
6. What end of *The Wind* did Lillian Gish prefer to have?
7. Why did Lillian Gish Leave MGM?
8. Why did auther say that five "Thalberg men" were forerunners of the Hollywood line producer?

II. Fill in the Blanks with the Words Given Below.

Characters in a fictional film naturally reveal a great deal about themselves by ( ) they say. But a great deal is also revealed by ( ) they say it. Their true thoughts, attitudes, and emotions can be revealed in ( ) way through word choice and through the stress, pitch, and pause patterns of their ( ). Actors' use of grammar, sentences structure, vocabulary, and particular ( ) reveals a great deal about their characters' social and ( ) level, educational background, and mental ( ). therefore, we must develop a keen ear, attuned to the faintest and most subtle nuances of meaning revealed through the the human voice.

There is an inner world of action that normally remains unseen and unheard by even the most careful observer/listener. Inner action ( ) within characters' minds and emotions. The most obvious way in which the filmmaker reveals inner reality is by taking us visually or aurally into the character's mind so that we see or hear the things that the character imagines, remembers, or thinks about. This may be achieved through a sustained ( ) view or through fleeting glimpses revealed by means of ( ).

a. economic b. subtle c. eternal d. processes e. how f. interior g. what
h. exceeds i. occurs j. metaphors k. dialects l. speech

III. Translation.

Section A: Put the followings into Chinese.

1. These were employees whose talents could not be easily defined and cultivated, who could not be trained and regulated like other craftsmen and technicians. But as important as they were to feature filmmaking, they had precious little control over their individual careers or their pictures.

2. Mayer in fact had rather significant battles in 1927—1928 with two top stars, Greta Garbo and Lillian Gish, and each of those skirmishes was revealing

of the star's authority at MGM and of the complex interplay of star persona and studio style.

3. Mayer caved in not only because of Garbo's market value and star appeal, but also because her screen persona was so well suited to MGM's prestige strategy and emerging high-gloss style which favored romantic melodrama and light comedy set in a contemporary milieu populated by glamorous, sophisticated characters.

4. Lillian Gish provided an interesting counterpoint to Garbo. She came to the studio an established star, but one whose personality was distinctly at odds with MGM's style and whose degree of control over the production process.

5. This required meticulous scheduling and script development, close collaboration with the various department heads to ensure efficiency and to maintain production values, and careful supervision of each picture.

Section B: Put the followings into English.

对大众来说，好莱坞仍然存在（尽管它在很大程度上已经名存实亡了），他们相信电影是为大众娱乐服务的。对于历史学家来说，好莱坞电影其实只存在于一段特定的时期。现在大家所熟知的经典好莱坞电影，指的是20世纪初到20世纪60年代早期在制片厂制度下所制作的电影。环球、米高梅、派拉蒙、华纳兄弟及哥伦比亚是独立的电影制片厂，它们有自己的制片设备、导演、制片人、制作部门和一大批固定演员。

Text B

Still 2-1

Still 2-2

Casablanca

para 1 *Casablanca* begins with the Warner Brothers shield logo and theme music. This was on every film distributed by the studio. The system identified the company that put out the product so the consumer would know what to expect. Each studio had a particular look and story philosophy. *Casablanca*, like the majority of studio films, was photographed in black and white, which allowed the viewer to enter the dream world on the screen. The system believed that black and white was a medium that could pull in the audience without distraction—it was a universe of the tonal scale from black to white, with shades of gray in between.

para 2 During the opening titles of *Casablanca,* Max Steiner's musical score sets the tone for exotic intrigue; right on cue, as his credit appears, the music proudly plays *La Marseillaise* to celebrate the glory of the

French World War II resistance movement, which will prevail by the conclusion of the film. The system relied heavily on almost wall-to-wall music to indicate setting , mood, and emotion.

para 3 At times an unidentified narrator sets the scene. In *Casablanca* a deep-throated male voice, one that could have been heard on the radio during the 1940s, explains the during the start of World War II, people traveled to Casablanca in French Morocco in hopes of flying to the freedom of democracy in the United States.

para 4 The musical score by Max Steiner is a classic of the era. The music underlines and often indicates the emotional state the audience should be in. There are two categories of film music. As labeled by film and film sound theorists, diegetic sound is sound that organically occurs within the frame. Sam's piano playing and singing, as well as other musical performances in *Casablanca* is classified as diegetic sound. Nondiegetic sound is not produced within the screen image. This applies to the musical underscore in *Casablanca*. The combination of diegetic and nondiegetic music in the film produces a powerful emotional state that speaks to the romance, memory sense, and patriotic fervor of *Casablanca*.

para 5 Characters are defined by their actions. Throughout the film, Renault is a bad good guy; he is on whatever side the wind blows and like many Hollywood characters he has a tough exterior, a glib mouth, and a good heart. Rick (Humphrey Bogart) appears to be a hard-bitten tough guy, but later rescues a young couple and secures their passage to America. Renualt tells him he's an old sentimentalist. There is even on two-shot that includes good and bad by framing Ilsa (Ingrid Bergman) on one side and Major Strasser (Conrad Veidt) on the other.

para 6 The famous last scene takes place at the airport. It is night and there is a dense fog, giving the illusion that we are seeing more than is really there. Rick becomes the hero and gives up the girl so that she can go on to America with her husband, a true hero. In return, for the first time Rick becomes whole, also a trued hero. He is welcomed back to the fight by the tricky Renault. What will happen to these men? A Nazi officer was murdered. Somehow they will both survive. It is the beginning of a beautiful friendship, a metaphor so rich with meaning it could only be in a film made by the Hollywood dream factory, in which a film reinvents itself in meaning to each passing generation and with each viewing, as time goes by.

I. Context Clues.

Guess the meanings of the following with the help of the context clues.

1. the majority of studio films ______________________________
2. a universe of the tonal scale ______________________________
3. exotic intrigue ______________________________
4. wall-to-wall music ______________________________
5. on whatever side the wind blows ______________________________
6. each passing generation ______________________________

II. Questions for Consideration.

1. Do you appreciate the almost wall-to-wall music which indicates setting, mood, and emotion in the film? Why?

2. Do you agree with the conception that *Casablanca* represents classical Hollywood film style? Why?

Unit Three

Text A

The Story of Westerns

para 1 Westerns are the major defining genre of the American film industry, a nostalgic eulogy to the early days of the expansive, untamed American frontier (the borderline between civilization and the wilderness). They are one of the oldest, most enduring and flexible genres and one of the most characteristically American genres in their mythic origins.

para 2 This indigenous American art form focuses on the frontier West that existed in North America. Westerns are often set on the American frontier during the last part of the 19th century (1865–1900) following the Civil War, in a geographically western (trans-Mississippi) setting with romantic, sweeping frontier landscapes or rugged rural terrain. However, Westerns may extend back to the time of America's colonial period or forward to the mid-20th century, or as far geographically as Mexico. A number of westerns use the Civil War, the Battle of the Alamo (1836) or the Mexican Revolution (1910) as a backdrop.

para 3 The Western genre sometimes portrays the conquest of the wilderness and the subordination of nature in the name of civilization or the confiscation of the territorial rights of the original, Native American, inhabitants of the frontier. The Western depicts a society organized around codes of honor and personal, direct or private justice—"frontier justice"—dispensed by gunfights. These honor codes are often played out through depictions of feuds or individuals seeking personal revenge or retribution against someone who has wronged them (e.g. *True Grit* has revenge and retribution as its main themes). This Western depiction of personal justice contrasts sharply with justice systems organized around rationalistic, abstract law that exist in cities, in which social order is maintained predominately through relatively impersonal institutions such as courtrooms.

para 4 The popular perception of the Western is a story that centers on the life of a semi-nomadic wanderer, usually a cowboy or a gunfighter. A showdown or duel at high noon featuring two or more gunfighters is a stereotypical scene in the popular conception of Westerns.

para 5 In some ways, such protagonists may be considered the literary descendants of the knight errant which stood at the center of earlier extensive genres such as the Arthurian Romances. Like the cowboy or gunfighter of the Western, the knight errant of the earlier European tales and poetry was wandering from place to place on his horse, fighting villains of various kinds and bound to no fixed social structures but only to his own innate code of honor. And like knights errant, the heroes of Westerns frequently rescue damsels in distress. Similarly, the wandering protagonists of Westerns share many characteristics with the ronin in modern Japanese culture.

para 6 The Western typically takes these elements and uses them to tell simple morality tales, although some notable examples (e.g. the later Westerns of John Ford or Clint Eastwood's *Unforgiven,* about an old hired killer) are more morally ambiguous. Westerns often stress the harshness and isolation of the wilderness and frequently set the action in an arid, desolate landscape. Specific settings include isolated forts, ranches and homesteads; the Native American village; or the small frontier town with its saloon, general store, livery stable and jailhouse and the open desert, where there are no structures and only windswept sand dunes. Apart from the wilderness, it is usually the saloon that emphasizes that this is the Wild West: it is the place to go for music (raucous piano playing), women (often prostitutes), gambling (draw poker or five card stud), drinking (beer or whiskey), brawling and shooting. In some Westerns, where civilization has arrived, the town has a church, a general store, a bank and a school; in others, where frontier rules still hold sway, it is, as Sergio Leone said, "where life has no value".

para 7 The American Film Institute defines Western films as those "set in the American West that embody the spirit, the struggle and the demise of the new frontier". The term Western, used to describe a narrative film genre, appears to have originated with a July 1912 article in *Moving Picture World* magazine. Most of the characteristics of Western films were part of 19th century popular Western fiction and were firmly in place before film became a popular art form. Western films commonly feature protagonists such as cowboys, gunslingers, and bounty hunters, who are often depicted as semi-nomadic wanderers who wear Stetson hats, bandannas, spurs, and buckskins, use revolvers or rifles as everyday tools of survival—and as a means to settle disputes using "frontier justice". Protagonists ride between dusty towns and cattle ranches on their trusty steeds.

para 8 Western films were enormously popular in the silent film era (1894–1927). With the advent of sound in 1927–1928, the major Hollywood studios rapidly abandoned Westerns, leaving the genre to smaller studios and producers. These smaller organizations churned out countless low-budget features and serials in the 1930s. By the late 1930s, the Western film was widely regarded as a "pulp" genre in

Hollywood, but its popularity was dramatically revived in 1939 by major studio productions such as *Dodge City* starring Errol Flynn, *Jesse James* with Tyrone Power, *Union Pacific* with Joel McCrea, *Destry Rides Again* featuring James Stewart and Marlene Dietrich, and the release of John Ford's landmark Western adventure *Stagecoach,* which became one of the biggest hits of the year. Released through United Artists, *Stagecoach* made John Wayne a mainstream screen star in the wake of a decade of headlining B westerns. Wayne had been introduced to the screen ten years earlier as the leading man in director Raoul Walsh's widescreen *The Big Trail*, which failed at the box office, due in part to exhibitors' inability to switch over to widescreen during the Depression. After the Western's renewed commercial successes in the late 1930s, the popularity of the Western continued to rise until its peak in the 1950s, when the number of Western films produced outnumbered all other genres combined.

para 9 Western films often depict conflicts with Native Americans. While early Eurocentric Westerns frequently portray the "steadicam" as dishonorable villains, the later and more culturally neutral Westerns gave Native Americans a more sympathetic treatment. Other recurring themes of Westerns include Western treks (e.g. *The Big Trail*) or perilous journeys (e.g. *Stagecoach*) or groups of bandits terrorising small towns such as in *The Magnificent Seven*. Or revisionist westerns like *I Walk the Line* (1970) depict sheriffs dueling.

para 10 Early Westerns were mostly filmed in the studio, just like other early Hollywood films, but when location shooting became more common from the 1930s, producers of Westerns used desolate corners of Arizona, California, Colorado, Kansas, Montana, Nevada, New Mexico, Oklahoma, Texas, Utah, or Wyoming. These settings gave filmmakers the ability to depict vast plains, looming mountains and epic canyons. Productions were also filmed on location at movie ranches.

para 11 Often, the vast landscape becomes more than a vivid backdrop; it becomes a character in the film. After the early 1950s, various wide screen formats such as cinemascope (1953) and Vista Vision used the expanded width of the screen to display spectacular Western landscapes. John Ford's use of Monument Valley as an expressive landscape in his films from *Stagecoach* (1939) to *Cheyenne Autumn* (1965) "present us with a mythic vision of the plains and deserts of the American West, embodied most memorably in Monument Valley, with its buttes and mesas that tower above the men on horseback, whether they be settlers, soldiers, or Native Americans".

Screen for Reference

Stagecoach（《关山飞渡》，1939 年）

The Treasure of the Sierra Madre（《浴血金沙》，1948 年）

High Noon（《正午》，1952 年）

The Good, the Bad and the Ugly（《黄金三镖客》，1966 年）

Dances with Wolves（《与狼共舞》，1990 年）

New Words

nostalgic /nɒ'stældʒɪk/ *adj.*

feeling, evoking, or characterized by nostalgia; asentimental longing or wistful affection for a period in the past 怀旧的；乡愁的

eulogy /'juːlədʒi/ *n.*

a speech or piece of writing that praises someone or something highly, especially a tribute to someone who has just died 颂词，赞词，悼词

untamed /ˌʌn'temd/ *adj.*

not domesticated or otherwise controlled 不能抑制的，未驯服的

indigenous /ɪn'dɪdʒənəs/ *adj.*

originating or occurring naturally in a particular place; native 国产的，固有的；本土的，土著的

backdrop /'bækdrɑːp/ *n.*

a painted cloth hung at the back of a theatre stage as part of the scenery 背景，背景幕

subordination /səˌbɔːdɪ'neɪʃn/ *n.*

the action of subordinating or the state of being subordinate 从属，附属，主从关系

retribution /ˌretrɪ'bjuːʃn/ *n.*

punishment inflicted on someone as vengeance for a wrong or criminal act 报应，惩罚，报偿

rationalistic /ˌræʃnə'lɪstɪk/ *adj.*

of or relating to the philosophical doctrine of rationalism 理性主义的，纯理论的

predominate /prɪ'dɒmɪneɪt/ *v.*

be the strongest or main element; be greater in number or amount 支配，主宰；在……中占有优势

errant /'erənt/ *adj.*

erring or straying from the accepted course or standards 不定的，周游的，错误的，偏离正路的

Phrase and Expression

the advent of

the approach or arrival of ……的出现，……的到来

I. Reading Comprehension.

1. What is the origin of westerns?
2. What the backdrop for western films was usually used?
3. What is the theme of the westerns?
4. What is a stereotypical scene in the popular conception of Westerns?
5. Why are the westerns protagonists considered the literary descendants of the knight?
6. How do westerns make an atmosphere for showing the harshness and isolating of the wilderness?
7. What art form shared its characteristics for westerns, and how did it shape its figures and action in films according to the author?
8. What is the advantage of location shooting for westerns compared with being filmed in the studio and why?

II. Fill in the Blanks with the Words Given Below.

The director can ( ) on another characteristic of color to ensure that attention is attracted to the proper object: Some colors seem to advance toward the foreground, and others seem to recede into the background. Colors such as red, orange, yellow, and ( ) are ( ) colors. When given high intensity and dark value, they seem to ( ), making objects appear larger and closer to the camera than they are. Interior decorators and others know that a chair covered in red will seem larger and closer to an observer than the same chair covered in ( ) colors such ( ), green , or pale blue. Taking advantage of the characteristics of color fosters the illusion that the image on the screen is three-dimensional.

Several other techniques may be used in a color film to create the illusion of different ( ) of depth. By controlling the lighting and color choices, the director can ( ) or accent the illusion of solidity. Colors convey or at least seem to convey a sense of ( ). The generalizations are not without certain ( ).

Filmmakers are aware of these connotations and use them to good effect.

a. complication	b. capitalize	c. advanced	d. lavender	e. planes	f. receding
g. advancing	h. dramatize	i. advance	j. beige	k. temperature	l. saturated

III. Translation.

Section A: Put the followings into Chinese.

1. However, Westerns may extend back to the time of America's colonial period or forward to the mid-20th century, or as far geographically as Mexico. A number of westerns use the Civil War, the Battle of the Alamo (1836) or the Mexican Revolution (1910) as a backdrop.

2. The Western genre sometimes portrays the conquest of the wilderness and the subordination of nature in the name of civilization or the confiscation of the territorial rights of the original, Native American, inhabitants of the frontier.

3. This Western depiction of personal justice contrasts sharply with justice systems organized around rationalistic, abstract law that exist in cities, in which social order is maintained predominately through relatively impersonal institutions such as courtrooms.

4. Like knights errant, the heroes of Westerns frequently rescue damsels in distress. Similarly, the wandering protagonists of Westerns share many characteristics with the ronin in modern Japanese culture.

5. The term Western, used to describe a narrative film genre, appears to have originated with a July 1912 article in *Moving Picture World* magazine.

Section B: Put the followings into English.

通过这部电影，这个创造出了西部电影史诗神话的人，转向了美国历史中黑暗的、不为人知的领域。在荷马、莎士比亚和弗洛伊德的精神启发下，约翰·福特为美国电影史的新篇章奠定了基础。

电影发生在1868年的得克萨斯州。《搜索者》的开场和结尾都是从室内拍向纪念谷的视野。风景栩栩如生，有蓝天、深珊瑚色的群山、浅色的黄土及绿色的灌木。

Text B

Still 3-1

Still 3-2

The Searchers

para 1 The screen story and thematic intentions of John Ford's (1895–1973) *The Searchers* have over time certified this 1956 American Western as one of the most influential movies of the modern era. Since the 1970s, *The Searchers* has been considered by critics internationally to be among the finest of the Western genre. *The Searchers* resonates because it tackles universal issues: the search for home, racial differences, the obsessions of love, hate, and vengeance, and the complex nature of the id. *The Searchers* is also a well-told tale with multifaceted characters that brims with conflict, plenty of action, dramatic meditation, warmth, and humor.

para 2 John Ford considered himself not a filmmaker, but a film director. The difference may be semantics, but Ford was not a hands-on filmmaker such as Alfred Hitchcock, King Vidor, or Orson Welles. John Ford was a classicist, a Hollywood professional, and a cinematic poet. He directed with personal vision and by leadership. The insightful thematic treatment and engaging story sensibilities of *The Searchers* are translated and structured by images that serve their purpose with unpretentious virtue. Each shot is composed and staged to convey a sense of place, emotional truth, and dramatic fulfillment. Ford rarely moves the camera. when he tracks alongside the gallop of horseback riders or pushes in for a close-up, it is for a reason that has nothing to do with personal visual style and everything to do with applying the right technique for that moment in the story. There is a minimum of interscene editing. Ford cuts only when it is absolutely necessary to move to another view or angle. His choices are only dictated by the story he is telling, not artistic ego or personal expression. *The Searchers* may be John Ford's most personal film in which he probed the American psyche, but it is also a well-made movie, a paradigm for the classical style of the American film.

para 3 John Ford was a master cinematic storyteller. This strong narrative, abounding with insight into the human condition, is cinematically rendered with elegiac and potent moving images. Director of photography Winton C. Hoch shot *The Searchers* in technicolor and Vista Vision. The color is deeply saturated and especially rich in capturing the red, blue, green, and earth tones that define the Western genre. Vista Vision was widescreen process in which 35mm film ran through the camera horizontally rather than by the standard vertical flow to create an image with an approximate aspect ratio of 1:85:1, the standard widescreen format for American films. Vista Vision excelled in sharp definition. The extreme clarity of the process assisted Ford and Hoch in achieving a hyperrealism that expressed the extreme range of emotions attained by the characters in the story.

para 4 *The Searchers* made a lasting impression on the third generation of American film directors. The motifs of the nature of family, the racial politics of hate, and the journey for internal realization appeared in the work of many American New Wave filmmakers, emerging in many forms distilled by the perceptions of a diverse group who share respect for and a yearning to participate in Ford's search for the American character. Martin Scorsese's *Taxi Driver*, Steven Spielberg's *Close Encounters of the Third Kind*, George Lucas's *Star Wars*, and Michael Cimino's *The Deer Hunter* continued John Ford's tradition of making American films that go beyond genre conventions and speak to who we are as Americans.

I. Context Clues.

Guess the meanings of the following with the help of the context clues.

1. universal issues ______________________________

2. the complex nature of the id ______________________________

3. multifaceted characters ______________________________

4. hands-on filmmaker ______________________________

5. unpretentious virtue ______________________________

II. Questions for Consideration.

1. How is *The Searchers* valued by critics internationally?

2. Why did John Ford consider himself not a filmmaker, but a film director?

Unit Four

Text A

The Modernity of Cinema

para 1 Accepting that the common ground in all definitions of artistic modernism is that modern art is an aesthetic reflection on and a critique of its own traditional forms, cinematic modernism is a special case when compared to other forms of modern art. During at least the first sixty years of film history, one could not reasonably speak about a cinematic tradition whatsoever. Cinema as a cultural tradition was first invented by auteurs of the French new wave. Jean-Luc Godard says, "A contemporary writer knows that authors such as Molière or Shakespeare existed. We are the first filmmakers who know that a D. W. Griffith existed. At the time when Marcel Carné, Louis Delluc, and René Clair made their first films, there was no critical or historical tradition yet". Obviously, the modernism of the 1920s could not be a "reflection on cinema's own artistic traditions".

para 2 In the early 1920s, clear ideas emerged in film criticism about what "real" cinema should be like, and with that an intensive critique of a kind of theatrical "artistic" mass production of European films. The main factor in the emergence of early modernism during the 1920s was not a critical reaction against the narrative standards that were just becoming norms. Some theoreticians and critics of early modern cinema considered emulating even the realist, linear, and continuous narration of the American model. Far from opposing the "Hollywood norm", Delluc, a prominent figure of early French modernism, remarked in 1921 that the real film drama was created by American cinema, and he called on the French to follow this way of filmmaking. Similarly, Soviet filmmaker Dziga Vertov criticized the "Germano-Russian" theatrical style and praised American narrative films for their dynamism, speed, and their use of close-ups. The rise of late modernism in the 1950s witnessed the same relationship of modern European filmmakers to classical American cinema. French new wave critics of the *Cahiers du cinéma* attacked not Hollywood films or narrative in general, but—in the words of Truffaut, "a certain tendency of French cinema". Just like some thirty years earlier, the action-centered Hollywood narrative was an important inspiration for late modern cinema, as opposed to the "dead classicism" of European bourgeois middle-class drama, which had less to do with classical narrative norms than with nineteenth-century bourgeois theater.

para 3 Early modern filmmakers critiqued not so much popular narrative cinema as the artistic utilization of cinema, which they themselves were busy modernizing. Because cinema did not have an artistic tradition proper to its medium to modernize, there were different ways to achieve this goal. One way to bring out the artistic potential of cinema was to create cinematic versions of modernist movements in fine arts, theater, and literature, or simply fit cinema in with narrative and visual forms of the national cultural heritage. In this sense, early modernism was cinema's reflection on artistic or cultural traditions outside of the cinema. German expressionism was the first appearance of that kind of modernism in the cinema. Expressionism tried to organically apply extracinematic artistic means to cinema. No filmmaker before expressionism thought of doing this to such an extent, and nobody conceived of cinema as an art related to artistic modernism. The importance of expressionism in this respect is that it institutionalized cinema as a medium capable of modern visual abstraction.

para 4 Again, the modernity of expressionism is not to be found in how it differs from the canonized norms of narrative cinema. In fact, as far as narrative is concerned, German expressionist films were not at all subversive, and they respected most classical rules. The extremely unrealistic character of some of their narratives was probably unusual in Hollywood terms, but they were not at all anti-Hollywood in their principles. Expressionist films were in fact the first models of some of the most popular Hollywood genres, such as vampire and monster movies and psychothrillers. Even their unusual and extravagant visual devices turned out to be familiar to the Hollywood visual universe. On the one hand, the success of the German filmmakers who emigrated to Hollywood in the 1930s shows that their cinematic culture in fact harmonized well with the Hollywood way of thinking. On the other hand, the stylistic renewal of the American cinema by Orson Wells and film noir in the 1940s had its foundation precisely in expressionist cinematography. Later on, the formal principles of other modernist and avant-garde movements appeared in the cinema as well, such as surrealism, futurism, Dadaism and cubism. However, only expressionism and surrealism had a lasting impact on the development of cinema. But other experiments with modernist visual devices and sequential principles were also important to the institutionalization of cinema as a modern form of art.

para 5 Another aspect of early modernism's reflexive character was its search for the "pure" form of the cinema. While in the trend discussed above the rejection of the narrative function was not always a conscious choice, in the "pure cinema" trend of early modernism it was one of the main principles. Cinema was to be affirmed as an independent art form by isolating its tools from those of other art forms, especially literature and drama. The "absolute film" movement and other early forms of experimental cinema viewed film as a purely visual art in which literary and dramatic forms were not organic parts. This movement concentrated mainly on the technical aspects of the medium as the foundation of its aesthetic specificity. The representation and manipulation of movement, the articulation of time (rhythm), and the unusual association of images were the three main paths the "pure cinema" trend followed. By the end of the 1920s some of its representatives came to articulate this conception as an alternative to the "traditional" representation of reality. Walter Ruttman, Jean Vigo, but above all, Dziga Vertov applied "pure cinema" aesthetics to the construction of an image of reality that would be an alternative to that of classical narrative cinema.

Screen for Reference

Way Down East（《赖婚》，1920 年）
Dr. Mabuse, der Spieler（《玩家马布斯博士》，1922 年）
La Roue（《车轮》，1923 年）
Der Letzte Mann（《最卑贱的人》，1924 年）
Greed（《贪婪》，1924 年）

New Words

aesthetic /es'θetɪk/ *adj.*

concerned with beauty or the appreciation of beauty 美的，审美的

theoretician /ˌθɪərə'tɪʃn/ *n.*

a person who forms, develops, or studies the theoretical framework of a subject

理论家，精通于理论的人

emulate /'emjuleɪt/ *v.*

match or surpass (a person or achievement), typically by imitation 仿真，模仿；尽力赶上

bourgeois /ˌbʊr'ʒwɑː/ *adj.*

belonging to or characteristic of the middle class, typically with reference to its perceived materialistic values or conventional attitudes 资产阶级的，中产阶级的

heritage /'herɪtɪdʒ/ *n.*

property that has been or may be inherited by an heir 遗产，继承物

extravagant /ɪk'strævəgənt/ *adj.*

lacking restraint in spending money or using resources 奢侈的，浪费的，过度的，放纵的

sequential /sɪ'kwenʃl/ *adj.*

forming or following in a logical order or sequence 连续的，相继的，有顺序的

reflexive /rɪ'fleksɪv/ *adj.*

denoting a pronoun that refers back to the subject of the clause in which it is used 反身的，反射的

manipulation /məˌnɪpju'leɪʃn/ *n.*

the action of manipulating something in a skilful manner 操纵，操作，处理，篡改

Phrase and Expression

the emergence of

the process of becoming visible after being concealed ……的出现

bring out

produce or publish something; reveal something; make something clear or explicit 生产，出版；使显示；说出

I. Reading Comprehension.

1. Why is cinematic modernism a special case compared to other forms of modern art?
2. How does Delluc think of “Hollywood norm” ?
3. What did the author think of the way to achieve the modernity of cinema?
4. How did the article appraise the German expressionism?
5. What is the relationship between German expressionism and “Hollywood” ?
6. What modernist cinema movements have been mentioned in this article?
7. Which two art forms had a lasting impact on the development of cinema?
8. What were the three main paths the “pure cinema” trend followed?

II. Fill in the Blanks with the Words Given Below.

By the end of the 1910s, the Expressionism had gone from being a radical (   ) to being a widely accepted, even (   ) style. While the main defining traits of French Impressionism lay in the area of (   ), German Expressionism is distinctive primarily for its use of mise-en-scene. A crucial trait of Expressionist mise-en-scene is the (   ) of similar shapes within a composition.

From the most part, Expressionist films used simple lighting from the (   ) and sides, (   ) the scene flatly and evenly to stress the links between the figures and the decor.

Many Expressionist films have frame stories or (   ) stories embedded within the larger narrative structure. *Tartuffe* begins and ends with a frame story in which a young man tries to warm his aging father that the housekeeper is out to marry him for his money; his warning takes the form of a film of Moliere's play *Tartuffe*, which (   ) the inner story. In the cinema, Expressionism had the same potential for (   ) comment that it did on the stage. In most cases, however, filmmakers used the style to create exotic and fantastic settings that were remote from (   ) reality.

a. constitutes b. social c. fashionable d. experiment e. front f. conflictual
g. contemporary h. simultaneous i. self-contained j. juxtaposition k. illuminating
l. camerawork

III. Translation.

Section A: Put the followings into Chinese.

1. Accepting that the common ground in all definitions of artistic modernism is that modern art is an aesthetic reflection on and a critique of its own traditional forms, cinematic modernism is a special case when compared to other forms of modern art.

2. Obviously, the modernism of the 1920s could not be a "reflection on cinema's own artistic traditions".

3. French new wave critics of the *Cahiers du cinéma* attacked not Hollywood films or narrative in general, but—in the words of Truffaut, "a certain tendency of French cinema".

4. Expressionist films were in fact the first models of some of the most popular Hollywood genres, such as vampire and monster movies and psychothrillers.

5. Cinema was to be affirmed as an independent art form by isolating its

tools from those of other art forms, especially literature and drama.

Section B: Put the followings into English.

纵观影史，几乎没有什么影片能比德国默片《卡里加里博士的小屋》更能影响先锋电影、艺术电影或学生电影，该作品由罗伯特·维内执导，于1920年首映。这部75分钟的黑白影片开创了表现主义电影的先河，在使用电影这种媒介来关注抽象、情感或心理的可能性方面，它至今仍是创作者的灵感来源。

Text B

Still 4-1

Still 4-2

The Cabinet of Dr. Caligari

para 1 In expressionism traditional notions of realism are tossed aside for the exploration of distortion and exaggeration in shape and form, as opposed to figurative representation. Expressionism is abstract in nature, grotesque in its depiction of social and political power, and urgent in its authority to express the fervent emotions experienced by the artist.

para 2 German Expressionism began before World War I when a group of bohemian artists who all shared a sense of imminent disaster formed Die Brüke (The Bridge) in Munich. Led by Ludwig Kirchner. they were inspired to revive German art by reaching back to the early primitives. To achieve a contemporary approach to art, they were deliberately clumsy in their draftsmanship, which was dominated by bold black lines rather than the naturalistic modeling practiced by figurative artists. The paintings were brooding with forbidding elements of violence and sexual tension. German Expressionism was the fashion of the avant-garde and was despised by Adolph Hitler's Nazi party that suppressed it in 1933 as degenerate art.

para 3 The narrative logic of *The Cabinet of Dr. Caligari* is distorted as if it were a nightmare. It can be seen as a parable portraying a world in which evil is a constant presence winning over the struggle for rationality. The expressionist style is prevalent throughout *The Cabinet of Dr. Caligari*, including the opening scene. If the story were just a nightmare, there would be a stylistic separation between scenes of the real world and the dream world, and the narrative would be resolved when the sleeper awoke. Weine, like the German expressionist painters, was reflecting his emotional reaction to the world around him, which draws the viewer into a trance state from which there is no awakening through the duration of the film. In many ways *The Cabinet of Dr. Caligari* is a horror film with the mad scientist figure, a monster, murder, and an atmosphere of relentless fear. A social or political read of the film reveals an analogy to the moral and physical breakdown of Germany at the time, with a madman on the loose reeking havoc on a distorted and off-balanced society, a metaphor for a country in chaos.

para 4 The acting style is as emotionally over the top as the narrative and visual style of *The Cabinet of Dr. Caligari*. The behavior of the characters represents the actors' emotional responses to the expressionistic environment and the situations in which they find themselves. Staging and movement of the actors responds to the hysteria of Caligari's machinations and to the fun-house labyrinth that appears to be the reflection of a crazy mirror, not an orderly village. The characters exist in and respond to the twisted streets, rooms with radically offset windows, doors that are not squared, and chairs that are too tall. Buildings are clustered and interconnected by a cubist take on architecture in the city where they reside, which has been transformed by evil.

I. Context Clues.

Guess the meanings of the following with the help of the context clues.

1. distortion ________________________________
2. figurative representation ____________________
3. trance ___________________________________
4. in chaos _________________________________
5. hysteria _________________________________
6. labyrinth ________________________________

II. Questions for Consideration.

1. How do you understand the statement "The narrative logic of *The Cabinet of Dr. Caligari* is distorted as if it were a nightmare"?

2. What did the film reveal from social and political read?

Unit Five

Text A

What We Discover in the Close-Up

para 1 The first new world discovered by the film camera in the days of the silent film was the world of very small things visible only from very short distances, the hidden life of little things. By this the camera showed us not only hitherto unknown objects and events: the adventures of beetles in a wilderness of blades of grass, the tragedies of day-old chicks in a corner of the poultry-run, the erotic battles of flowers and the poetry of miniature landscapes. It brought us not only new themes. By means of the close-up the camera in the days of the silent film revealed also the hidden mainsprings of a life which we had thought we already knew so well. Blurred outlines are mostly the result of our insensitive short-sightedness and superficiality.

para 2 We skim over the teeming substance of life. The camera has uncovered that cell-life of the vital issues in which all great events are ultimately conceived: for the greatest landslide is only the aggregate of the movements of single particles. A multitude of close-ups can show us the very instant in which the general is transformed into the particular. The close-up has not only widened our vision of life, it has also deepened it. In the days of the silent film it not only revealed new things, but showed us the meaning of the old.

para 3 The close-up can show us a quality in a gesture of the hand we never noticed before when we saw that hand stroke or strike something, a quality which is often more expressive than any play of the features. The close-up shows your shadow on the wall with which you have lived all your life and which you scarcely knew; it shows the speechless face and fate of the dumb objects that live with you in your room and whose fate is bound up with your own. Before this you looked at your life as a concert-goer ignorant of music listens to an orchestra playing a symphony. All he hears is the leading melody, all the rest is blurred into a general murmur. Only those can really understand and enjoy the music who can hear the contrapuntal architecture of each part in the score. This is how we see life: only its leading melody meets the eye. But a good film with its close-ups reveals the most hidden parts in our polyphonous life, and teaches us to see the intricate visual details of life as one reads an orchestral score.

para 4 The close-up may sometimes give the impression of a mere naturalist preoccupation with detail. But good close-ups radiate a tender human attitude in the contemplation of hidden things, a delicate solicitude, a gentle bending over the intimacies of life-in-the miniature, a warm sensibility. Good close-ups are lyrical; it is the heart, not the eye, that has perceived them.

para 5 Close-ups are often dramatic revelations of what is really happening under the surface of appearances. You may see a medium shot of someone sitting and conducting a conversation with icy calm. The close-up will show trembling fingers nervously fumbling a small object—sign of an internal storm. Among pictures of a comfortable house breathing a sunny security, we suddenly see the evil grin of a vicious head on the carved mantelpiece or the menacing grimace of a door opening into darkness. Like the leitmotif of impending fate in an opera, the shadow of some impending disaster falls across the cheerful scene.

para 6 Close-ups are the pictures expressing the poetic sensibility of the director. They show the faces of things and those expressions on them which are significant because they are reflected expressions of our own subconscious feeling. Herein lies the art of the true cameraman.

para 7 In a very old American film I saw this dramatic scene: the bride at the altar suddenly runs away from the bridegroom whom she detests, who is rich and who has been forced on her. As she rushes away she must pass through a large room full of wedding presents. Beautiful things, good things, useful things, things radiating plenty and security smile at her and lean towards her with expressive faces. And there are the presents given by the bridegroom: faces of things radiating touching attention, consideration, tenderness, love—and they all seem to be looking at the fleeing bride, because she looks at them; all seem to stretch out hands towards her, because she feels they do so. There are ever more of them—they crowd the room, and block her path—her flight slows down more and more, then she stops and finally turns back...

para 8 Having discovered the soul of things in the close-up, the silent film undeniably overrated their importance and sometimes succumbed to the temptation of showing "the hidden little life" as an end in itself, divorced from human destinies; it strayed away from the dramatic plot and presented the "poetry of things" instead of human beings. But what Lessing said in his *Laocoön* about Homer—that he never depicted anything but human actions and always described objects only inasmuch as they took part in the action—should to this day serve as a model for all epic and dramatic art as long as it centers around the presentation of man.

para 9 Every art deals with human beings, it is a human manifestation and presents human beings. To paraphrase Marx: "The root of all art is man." When the film close-up strips the veil of our imperceptiveness and insensitivity from the hidden little things and shows us the face of objects, it still shows us man, for what makes objects expressive are the human expressions projected on to them. The objects only reflect our own selves, and this is what distinguished art form scientific knowledge. When we see the face of things, we do what the ancients did in creating gods in man's image and breathing a human soul into them. The close-up of the film are the creative instruments of this mighty visual anthropomorphism.

Screen for Reference

The Passion of Joan of Arc（《圣女贞德蒙难记》，1928 年）
Pickpocket（《扒手》，1959 年）
Husbands（《夫君》，1970 年）

New Words

hitherto /ˌhɪðə'tuː/ *adv.*
so far 迄今为止
miniature /'mɪnɪtʃər/ *adj.*
very small 微型的，小规模的
mainspring /'meɪnsprɪŋ/ *n.*
chief motive or reason for something 主要动力，主发条；主要原因，主要动机
blurred /blɜːrd/ *adj.*
indistinct or hazy in outline 模糊不清的，被弄污的

superficiality /ˌsjuːpəˌfɪʃiˈæləti/ *n.*

shallowness; shallowness in terms of affecting only surface layers of something 浅薄，肤浅；表面性的事物

teeming /ˈtiːmɪŋ/ *adj.*

abounding 丰富的，热闹的

aggregate /ˈægrɪgət/ *n.*

a sum total of many heterogenous things taken together; a total 集合体，聚集

multitude /ˈmʌltɪˌtjuːd/ *n.*

extremely large number of things or people 多数，大批

dumb /dʌm/ *adj.*

unable to speak 哑的，不能说话的

murmur /ˈmɜːmər/ *v.*

to say something in a soft quiet voice that is difficult to hear or understand 低语，喃喃细语

contrapuntal /ˌkɒntrəˈpʌntl/ *adj.*

having two or more tunes played together to form a whole 多曲调演奏的，复调音乐的

score /skɔː/ *n.*

a written form of a musical composition 配乐

polyphonous /pəˈlɪfənəs/ *adj.*

of or relating to characterized by polyphony 多音的，复调的

intricate /ˈɪntrəkət/ *adj.*

complicated or detailed 复杂的，错综的，缠结的

anthropomorphism /ˌænθrəpəˈmɔrfɪzəm/ *n.*

the attribution of a human form, human characteristics, or human behavior to nonhuman things 拟人论，神人同形同性论

Phrases and Expressions

skim over

move or pass swiftly and lightly over the surface of; read superficially 掠过，

滑过；浏览

bound up with

closely connected with something 与……关系密切

I. Reading Comprehension.

1. By means of the close-up what categories does the camera reveal us?
2. What does close-up mean to the new things and the old?
3. How does the author stress the quality in a close-up shot in the third paragraph?
4. How do you understand the statement "All he hears is the leading melody, all the rest is blurred into a general murmur"?
5. What does architecture in the passage mean?
6. What else can we see in our life on top of leading melody?
7. What does the close-up illustrate the emotion of the director?
8. Why does the author say what makes objects expressive are the human expressions projected on to them in the last paragraph?

II. Fill in the Blanks with the Words Given Below.

The style of the Impressionist movement ( ) partly from the director's beliefs about the cinema as an art form. They expressed these beliefs in poetic, often abstruse, essays and ( ), which helped ( ) them as a distinct group.

The Impressionists saw art as a form of expression, ( ) the personal vision of the artist: art creates an experience, and that experience leads to ( ) for the spectator. Art creates these feelings not by making direct statements but by ( ) or suggesting them. In short, artworks create fleeting feelings, or impressions. By the 1920s, this view of art was a bit old-fashioned, being rooted in nineteenth-century Romantic and ( ) aesthetics.

Of the ( ) European movements that overlapped during the 1920s, French Impressionism lasted the longest, from 1918 to early 1929. Late in the decade, several factors ( ) to its decline. As the movements became better established, the interests of its filmmakers became more diverse. In addition, significant changes within the French film industry made it more difficult for some of them to ( ) control over their own work.

a. evoking b. emotions c. define d. two e. conveying f. retain g. contributed h. Symbolist i. derived j. manifestos k. dominated l. three

III. Translation.

Section A: Put the followings into Chinese.

1. By means of the close-up the camera in the days of the silent film revealed also the hidden mainsprings of a 1ife which we had thought we already knew so well.

2. The camera has uncovered that cell-life of the vital issues in which all great events are ultimately conceived.

3. A multitude of close-ups can show us the very instant in which the general is transformed into the particular.

4. All he hears is the leading melody, all the rest is blurred into a genera1 murmur. Only those can really understand and enjoy the music who can hear the contrapuntal architecture of each part in the score. This is how we see life: only its leading melody meets the eye.

5. Having discovered the soul of things in the close-up, the silent film undeniably overrated their importance and sometimes succumbed to the temptation of showing "the hidden little life" as an end in itself, divorced from human destinies.

Section B: Put the followings into English.

德·西卡使用的戏剧技巧与阿尔弗雷德·希区柯克或约翰·福特这样的导演比起来并没有什么特别，这种戏剧技巧依托于叙事的开展。电影一开场，安东尼在自行车被偷之前表现了对预言师的轻蔑态度，而与此相对应的则是在影片结尾处，安东尼和布鲁诺转而向她寻求帮助的无可奈何。那个女人所预言的"今日无果，则永生不见"提升了观众的期待，凸显了以失败告终的悲剧性。

Text B

Still 5-1

Still 5-2

The Bicycle Thief

para 1 *The Bicycle Thief*, directed by Vittorio De Sica (1902–1974), is one of the most celebrated examples of Italian neorealism, a post-World War II film movement active in Italy from 1944 through 1953. The principal creators of the style were screenwriter Cesare Zavattini and directors Roberto Rossellini, Luchino Visconti, and De Sica. The influence of neorealism spread to the work of Federico Fellini, Michelangelo Antonioni, and Alberto Lattuda.

para 2 The directorial approach to this film as conceptual and controlled as any dramatic fiction film. *The Bicycle Thief* is not an example of a documentary style applied to fiction such as is brilliantly realized in *The Battle of Algiers* (Gillo Pontecorvo, 1966). This distinction between *The Bicycle Thief* and traditonal drama lies in the use of nonactors and in the devotion to a narrative that reflects and embraces unvarnished realism. The entire cast is completely believable. Casting was a painstaking process. De Sica's performers were from the working class being portrayed on the screen. They not only had the look of authenticity, but were able to take direction, repeat actions, and transmit their internal truths to the camera. Whereas trained actors will use technique to indicate the emotions, feelings, and action of characters they are playing, nonactors have life experience and a physicality that is their own—not an artistic creation.

para 3 De Sica employs the visual power and simplicity of silent cinema. When Antonio's wife, Maria (Lianella Carell), hocks her marriage bed sheets tucked in a bag, as the clerk takes them a tilt-up reveals shelves to the ceiling of hundreds of the same. This one shot poetically communicates the dire situation of the Italian working class. The intercutting between Bruno, who has been ordered by his father to go home by bus, and Antonio, who has decided he will steal a lone bike propped up against a wall, is pure visual storytelling. As soon as Antonio makes the fateful grab, the owner appears. After a chase Antonio is harassed and beaten by locals. The man has pity when he looks at the humiliation Antonio has suffered and the shame on Bruno's face. This masterfully directed sequence ends with a shot that defines the difference between American and international cinema. Both father and son walk off and are lost in the crowd as the sun falls. They continue to walk away from the camera. There is no next shot, no last minute twist—this is life as it is. In reality happy endings are rare. The bike is lost forever, but Bruno and Antonio have come together. The family is strong—the struggle for work and survival goes on.

para 4 *The Bicycle Thief* is a reminder that drama is embedded in the streets and in the lives of the lower classes, who fight against poverty, bureaucracy, and systems both political and financial that use entertainment to cover up social problems so they can maintain status quo. Neorealism is also a testament that artistry can reproduce life in ways that nonfiction cannot. Emotion is the tool. The open, honest actor can encapsulate and deliver dramatic reality that filmmakers must face if not to be relegated to a future of tinsel-town fantasies.

I. Context Clues.

Guess the meanings of the following with the help of the context clues.

1. the look of authenticity ______________________

2. the fateful grab ______________________

3. last minute twist ______________________

4. maintain status quo ______________________

5. relegate ______________________

II. Questions for Consideration.

1. What are the qualities that nonactors own?

2. Of what does *The Bicycle Thief* remind us according to the writer in 4th paragraph of the article?

Unit Six

Text A

The Long Take

para 1 Long take filmmaking is crucially bound up with developments in technology. In early cinema, and particularly in the film studio, the static camera prevailed. As editing gradually became the norm, the "tableau" Style of static long takes remained in use and achieved extraordinary eloquence in the hands of directors such as Feuillade and Sjostrom, but with pan/tilt heads, wheeled camera supports of several kinds, and the development of cranes and other means of raising the camera, long takes with camera movement became more feasible, although they could involve formidable technical difficulty. Lutz Bacher's *The Mobile Mise en Scène* (1978)—originally (and impressively) an MA thesis—is devoted to "the theory and practice of long-take camera movement". Among its numerous interests is a detailed history of the technological advances in grip equipment, dollies, and cranes between the 1920s and 1970s, which captures the ambitions and inventiveness of numerous cinematographers, directors, camera operators, and grips.

para 2 Zoom lenses enabled filmmakers to change the field of view without physically moving the camera. Initially featured in US television news and sports coverage, and in TV drama in the years after World War II, Rossellini was one feature film director who took up its use in the 1950s, but the zoom became extensively used in Hollywood production in the 1960s and 1970s. Zooming could be a much cheaper alternative to the track or dolly shot, though it also had very different optical effects. Beginning in the 1970s, the introduction of the Steadicam was decisive in making possible virtuoso long takes with elaborate camera movement that would have been impossible a few years before [among the most frequently cited examples shot on film are Stanley Kubrick's *The Shining*(1980), Henry and Karen's entry into the Copacabana nightclub in Martin Scorsese's *Goodfellas* (1990), and the opening of Robert Altman's *The Player* (1992)]. Coupled with the digital camera, Steadicam long takes have become longer and more elaborate. The shot that Sean O'Sullivan calls "the most celebrated long take in the history of American television"—the remarkably intricate shot of almost six minutes from the fourth instalment of the first season of *True Detective* (2014)—was achieved by shooting digitally even though the rest of the series was shot on film. Freed from the limitations imposed by the length of film a camera could hold, in principle shots can become endless. *Timecode* (Mike Figgis, 2000), *Russian Ark* (Aleksandr Sokurov, 2002), and most recently *Victoria* (Sebastian Schipper, 2015) consist of shots that last the entire length of these feature-length films.

para 3 Other dimensions of digital technology have introduced even more significant change. Live action cinema has always drawn on special effects of one kind or another, in both shooting and post-production, but on the whole the ontology of photography—the fundamental link between what is in front of the camera and what it records-remained. With computed-generated imagery(CGI) and digital compositing that indexical link is broken, or at least transformed: images—often of astonishing realism—can be produced that mimic the traditional relationship between "the camera" and its subject, but that did not originate in the traditional way. Here the prodigious physical effort and ingenuity that were involved in producing some of the most famous long takes in film history—for example, Alfred Hitchcock's *Rope*(1948) and Orson Welles's *Touch of Evil*(1958)—is in part replaced by the hugely time-consuming labour and inventiveness of programmers and compositors [for instance, the football stadium sequence in *The Secret in Their Eyes* (Juan José Campanella, 2009)]. Significant debates have arisen over long takes achieved by such methods but creating the impression of the traditional continuities of time, space, action, and camera. What importance, if any, should be attached to these differences in the processes of critical analysis and evaluation? D. N. Rodowick outlines the underlying change involved: "There is debate or discussion today because we are confronted with something new in the image, something that disturbs the perceptual defaults of the chemically based analogical image. We confront something that looks like photography, and continues to serve many of its cultural functions. Yet a felt change is occurring, or perhaps has occurred, in our phenomenological relationship with these images. A subtle shifting of gears is taking place in our current ontology, in our relation to the world and to others, as mediated through technologically produced images."

para 4 These can become pressing issues as production on celluloid becomes a minority option and digital processes of various kinds dominate the field. Lisa Purse engages with aspects of this discussion. There are further dimensions of cinematic time and space to consider. As Brian Henderson argues, writing primarily about Murnau, Welles, and Ophuls, the long take rarely appears as a plan-séquence (a whole scene filmed in one shot), "but almost always in combination with some form of editing". He writes: "It is obvious that any long take shot of a sequence shot requires connection with another shot or shots to fill out the sequence. Thus a long take style necessarily involves long takes and cutting in combination." A good deal of Henderson's significant early essay in the field is devoted to what he calls the "intra-sequence" cut. This is to say that in the vast majority of cases, the continuities of time, space, and action that characterise long takes have their effect in relation both to the shots they are joined to by editing and to wider structures in the film, within which shots of extended duration may have a more or less substantial place. Even in *Rope*, where shot transitions between long takes are in a number of cases disguised, straight cuts are built into the design (as they needed to be because of the length of film that projectors could hold prior to the introduction of platter systems in the 1980s).

para 5 Stephen Prince comments on the contrast between this traditional feature of the long take and the potential of digital filmmaking to abolish editing: "The power of the long takes employed by Kurosawa, Welles, and others lies in the way they open up a stylistic alternative in the body of a film whose editing does not rely on extended shots. Virtue lies in contrast. By removing contrast, the unbounded shot of *Russian Ark*, and its potential in digital cinema generally, poses as severe a threat as montage to the structural integrity of the shot in cinema."

para 6 Perhaps in such cases of "unbounded shots", neither "shot" nor "long take", with its inherently relative associations, is any longer an appropriate term.

Screen for Reference

Rope（《夺魂索》，1948 年）
Nostalgia（《乡愁》，1983 年）

The Time to Live and Time to Die（《童年往事》，1985 年）

New Words

static /'stætɪk/ *adj.*

lacking in movement, action, or change, especially in an undesirable or uninteresting way 静态的，静电的

tableau /'tæbləʊ/ *n.*

a group of models or motionless figures representing a scene from a story or from history 画面，活人画，戏剧性局面，生动的场面

formidable /'fɔːrmɪdəbl/ *adj.*

inspiring fear or respect through being impressively large, powerful, intense, or capable 强大的，可怕的，令人敬畏的

Steadicam /'stedɪˌkæm/ *n.*

a lightweight mounting for a film camera which keeps it steady for filming when handheld or moving 斯坦尼康摄影机稳定器

instalment /ɪn'stɔːlmənt/ *n.*

a sum of money due as one of several equal payments for something, spread over an agreed period of time; any of several parts of something which are published, broadcast, or made public in sequence at intervals（分期付款的）一期付款；（故事分段连载或连播等的）一集

ontology /ɑːn'tɑːlədʒi/ *n.*

the branch of metaphysics dealing with the nature of being; a set of concepts and categories in a subject area or domain that shows their properties and the relations between them 本体论；存在论

prodigious /prə'dɪdʒəs/ *adj.*

remarkably or impressively great in extent, size, or degree 惊人的，异常的，奇妙的，巨大的

ingenuity /ˌɪndʒə'njuːəti/ *n.*

the quality of being clever, original, and inventive 心灵手巧，独创性，精巧

duration /dju'reɪʃn/ *n.*

the time during which something continues 期间

Phrase and Expression

bound up with

closely connected with something 与……关系密切

in the hands of

in one' possession, control or care 由……掌握，在……掌握中

coupled with

link or associate somebody/something with somebody/something 加上，外加，与……相结合

draw on

do with; absorb; approach 利用，吸收，临近

I. Reading Comprehension.

1. What makes the long take filmmaking possible?
2. What assistance did filmmakers get from zoom lenses on the set?
3. Where was the zoom lens initially applied?
4. What is the most common example for Steadicam long take filmmaking?
5. What does something new in D. N. Rodowick words mean?
6. What does Brian Henderson think of the long takes?
7. How does the long take demonstrate its power in the view of Stephen Prince?
8. What do you think of the long takes after reading the article?

II. Fill in the Blanks with the Words Given Below.

Two different editing patterns have become more or less criterion in making (　) in time and space. The more conventional pattern, outside/in editing, follows a logical sequence and (　) on (　) us to the new setting. It allows us to move into a new setting from the outside and gradually work our way (　) to the details. The logical ( ) of each step is clearly shown so that we always know exactly where we are. We get our ( ) with an establishing shot of the whole setting, move into the setting itself, and then focus our attention on the details of the setting.

Inside/out editing does the exact ( ). We are jolted suddenly from a line of action that we completely understand to a close-up detail in a new and unfamiliar place. We don't know where we are or what is happening. Then, in a sequence of related shots, we back off from the detail of the first close-up and gradually find out where we are and what is happening. Thus, we move from a ( ) shot to distant, more ( ) shots that help us fully understand the action in the context of the new ( ).

a. transparence b. scene c. bearings d. concentrates e. general f. opposite
g. disorienting h. transitions i. cultivating j. context k.orienting l. inside

III. Translation.

Section A: Put the followings into Chinese.

1. Among its numerous interests is a detailed history of the technological advances in grip equipment, dollies, and cranes between the 1920s and 1970s, which captures the ambitions and inventiveness of numerous cinematographers, directors, camera operators, and grips.

2. Live action cinema has always drawn on special effects of one kind or another, in both shooting and post-production, but on the whole the ontology of photography—the fundamental link between what is in front of the camera and what it records-remained.

3. There is debate or discussion today because we are confronted with something new in the image, something that disturbs the perceptual defaults of the chemically based analogical image. We confront something that looks like photography, and continues to serve many of its cultural functions.

4. The long take rarely appears as a plan-séquence (a whole scene filmed in one shot), "but almost always in combination with some form of editing".

5. By removing contrast, the unbounded shot of *Russian Ark*, and its potential in digital cinema generally, poses as severe a threat as montage to the structural integrity of the shot in cinema.

Section B: Put the followings into English.

在撒切尔的视角中，在一个场景使用一个镜头的连续变化中，查尔斯长大了。他拒绝接受用他的蓝筹股去经营一家揭露丑闻的报社，这家报社损害到了前监护人的利益。撒切尔与查尔斯的权力对比，是先用一个极低的仰拍镜头，然后变成俯拍镜头被夸张地表现出来。在结尾的长镜头中，成年凯恩起身，变得比撒切尔高，表示了权力的更迭。

撒切尔的回忆到 1929 年结束。在一个固定的深焦镜头中，凯恩被告知他的报业公司由于股票市场崩溃已经破产了。凯恩和撒切尔分别在画面的两侧，查尔斯对撒切尔说，一直以来他都想要成为那种不受银行待见的人。

Text B

Still 6-1

Still 6-2

Citizen Kane

para 1 *Citizen Kane* might just be the great American movie of the twentieth century. This ambitious and innovative allegory, directed by Orson Welles (1915–1985) when he was only twenty-six years old, forged a bold, new cinematic language to atomize the life of Charles Foster Kane, a man who had, and then lost, everything because he could only offer or receive love on his won terms.

para 2 *Citizen Kane* opens with the final moments in the life of Charles Foster Kane (Orson Welles) and provides a clue to the mystery of why his flamboyant and extravagant life ended in loneliness. Through a series of dissolves the camera climbs up a number of fences that seclude a castle-like mansion set back on a lofty hill. As images of the massive estate slowly continue to fade in and fade out of one another, a private zoo, canal, bridge, and golf course are revealed. In the night fog, one gothic window is illuminated. The changing views get ever closer; then suddenly the light is extinguished. Now inside a bedroom, snowflakes pass through the air, a glass globe depicting a winter home setting is dropped out of a dying hand. The man's lips fill the screen as he utters his final words—"Rosebud".

para 3 "News on the March", a self-contained sequence, meticulously follows the form and style of a "March of Time" newsreel segment. The movie news obituary of Charles Foster Kane traces the creation and grandeur of his Xanadu manor, the global impact of his passing, his rise as a newspaper tycoon, the empire he built, the origin of his fortune and political sway, his personal and private life, a failed run for governor, the decline during the Great Depression, old age, and, finally, isolation without intimacy. A resonant announcer narrates with flowery prose, fashioning Kane as larger than life. Shots are quickly wiped off, replaced by thc next. The dissolve, iris, fade-in and out of black transitions—all structure and maintain the sequence at a brisk pace. Title cards and animated maps display information, multiplying the scope of Kane's influence. Footage is over and underexposed and scratched to achieve archival authenticity.

para 4 The sound of the closing musical fanfare grinds to a halt. A group of media men in a private screening room have been watching an incomplete version of an enigmatic life. Bright beams of light stream in from the projection room portals and paint the men in degrees of shadow and silhouette. The boss wants to know what made Kane tick. Their voices blare and overlap in the confined space. He assigns Thompson (Willian Alland), one of his reporters, to learn the significance of Kane's last words.

para 5 The inquiry begins at a nightclub owned by Susan Alexander (Dorothy Comingore), the second Mrs. Kane. During a lightning storm, the camera travels over a roof, then looks down through a rain-drenched skylight at the inebriated and despondent young woman. She refuses to talk to Thompson, who throughout the film is photographically and metaphorically in the dark about the key to Kane's psyche.

I. Context Clues.

Guess the meanings of the following with the help of the context clues.

1. allegory__________________________________

2. the camera climbs up a number of fences________________

3. gothic window________________________________

4. bright beams of light stream in____________________

5. the camera travels over a roof_____________________

II. Questions for Consideration.

1. What did Orson Welles create in this film to atomize the life of Charles Foster Kane?

2. What does the film *Citizen Kane* open with?

Unit Seven

Text A

Carl Theodor Dreyer

para 1 Carl Theodor Dreyer's nebulous and personally haunting childhood history began under the unassuming Danish registry name of Karl Nielsen, the infant son of an unmarried Swedish housekeeper named Josefine Bernhardine Nilsson whose placement in a Copenhagen private residence was curiously arranged by her employer, Carlsro landowner and horse breeder Jens Christian Torp, in the days before the baby's birth. The infant Nielsen would pass through two foster homes before being placed, at the age of nearly two, into the care of a Danish Lutheran typographer named Carl Theodor Dreyer and his wife, Inger Marie, and the child was subsequently given the adoptive father's name, Carl Theodor Dreyer. However, before the private adoption could be finalized, Nilsson, again carrying a child out of wedlock, consumed an accidentally fatal dose of phosphorous in the misguided belief of inducing a miscarriage. Consequently, the Dreyers were never properly compensated by Nilsson, as had been agreed upon, for adopting young Karl. Although it is uncertain when Dreyer discovered the circumstances surrounding his parentage, it is evident that the revelation had left an indelible mark on the gentle, intensely humble, and venerable filmmaker—a deep wound that Dreyer harbored privately, even as he summarily dismissed his childhood influences and parental estrangement in public appearances and interviews.

para 2 For his first film, Dreyer decided to film a banal melodrama that was selected more for logistical expediency than narrative merit entitled *The President* (1918). Rather than casting the studio actors employed by Nordisk, Dreyer followed his own artistic intuition and elected to assemble his own cast of professional and non-professional actors selected for their appropriate face types to the situational and psychological profile of the characters that they portray. From the onset, Dreyer dispensed with the artificiality of cosmetics and ornately decorated sets in order to achieve a naturalness and realism to his films.

para 3 The untimely death of his birth mother, Josephine, and the emotional distance of his adoptive mother, Inger Marie, would invariably manifest in Dreyer's highly idealized (and idealistic) characterization of the inexorably virtuous, self-sacrificing, and oppressed woman. Even before *The Passion of Joan of Arc* (1927) would irrevocably and misdirectedly categorize Dreyer as a director of cerebral, religious-themed art cinema, his early films already reflected his concern for the social status of women: Dame Margarete (Hildur Carlberg)'s graceful acceptance of the unalterable cycle of life in the poignant social comedy, *The Parson's Widow* (1921), Siri (Clara Pontoppidan)'s tragic response to an unwelcomed seduction in the Finnish Revolution episode of *Leaves from Satan's Book* (1919), Ida Frandsen (Astrid Holm)'s enabling, defensive rationalization of her husband's tyrannical behavior in the commercially successful domestic satire *Master of the House* (1925). However, despite the decidedly masculine titular reference of *Master of the House*, it is the abusive husband Viktor (Johannes Meyer)'s process of humbling and enlightenment at the influence of the three women in his life—his wife, Ida, his governess, Mads (Mathilde Nielsen), and his adolescent daughter, Karen (Karin Nellemose)—that provides the drama and humor for the film. *The President*, although presented from the point of view of a male protagonist, centers on the plight of the illegitimate daughter Victorine. In fact, Dreyer's compassion and innate concern for the suffering and repression of women would continue throughout his career: the oppressive inquisition of Joan in *The Passion of Joan of Arc*, Anne's emotionally devoid marriage in *Day of Wrath* (1943), and Gertrud's elusive search for ideal love in *Gertrud* (1964). Perhaps the most representative of Dreyer's feminine ideal, however, is not the inexhaustible conviction and impractical idealism of Joan or Gertrud, but Inger (Birgitte Federspiel)'s role in the Borgen household in *Ordet* (1954)—maternal, yet sensual; spiritual, yet practical; unshakable personal conviction, yet conciliatory and tolerant.

para 4 Inspired by the artistry and epic scope of D. W. Griffith's *The Birth of a Nation* (1915) and *Intolerance* (1916), Dreyer embarked on the large-scale production of *Leaves from Satan's Book*, a film adapted from *The Sorrows of Satan* by Marie Corelli. Similar in structure and thematic presentation to *Intolerance*, the film chronicles the destructive consequences of temptation on four historical events: the Crucifixion of Jesus Christ, the Spanish Inquisition, the French Revolution, and the Russo-Finnish War (an installment conceived by Dreyer that did not exist in the original Corelli book). Dissatisfied with the compromised end result of the critically unpopular Crucifixion episode, Dreyer, the consummate perfectionist, became consumed with the idea of re-shooting the life of Jesus of Nazareth in what would come to be known as Dreyer's obsession with the unrealized "Jesus film". It is important to note that despite the provocative and religious inference of the title, *Leaves from Satan's Book* is essentially a historical film that seeks to identify and present humanist concerns.

para 5 Dreyer's interest in creating historical adaptations, undoubtedly a consequence of his former career as a journalist, would perpetuate his reputation as a religious filmmaker when, after the popularity of *Master of the House* in France, the Société Général de Films approached Dreyer to make a historical drama, and Joan of Arc was selected over the other worthy subjects of Catherine de Medici and Marie Antoinette (who, like Jesus, was a prior character from *Leaves from Satan's Book*). As in his earlier films, Dreyer's primary interest was in capturing the indefinable essence of human suffering. In addition to the inherently religious and spiritually transcendent depiction of Joan (Renée Marie Falconetti)'s tragic and uncompromising ultimate sacrifice, Dreyer's humanist sentiment also transforms *The Passion of Joan of Arc* into a socially relevant and harrowing reflection of the senseless persecution of women in a patriarchal society. Moreover, by distilling the scope of the film to the trial process, Joan's oppressive environment and inescapable fate become acutely palpable. By concentrating on the physical toll of Joan's psychological ordeal, Dreyer translates the unattainable and resolute piety of Joan the saint into the accessible language of compassion for the pain and suffering of Joan the human, achieving a coexistent and symbiotic relationship between the metaphysical and the corporeal that Dreyer defines as realized mysticism.

para 6 In dispelling Dreyer's reputation as a director of religious films, the strangely atmospheric and ethereal landscape of *Vampyr* (1931) may be viewed not as a radical departure to his spiritual canon, but as a reflection of his propensity for experimentation. Influenced in part by the surrealist art movement pervasive in France at the time of his residence, and also by a deliberate compulsion to escape the stigma of being referred to as a "saint's director", Dreyer sought to make *Vampyr* an antithesis of *The Passion of Joan of Arc*: distanced, voluminous, dispassionate, and unemotive. Nevertheless, despite Dreyer's flourishing creativity and artistic achievement abroad, *Vampyr* was a commercial failure and led to the dissolution of his short-lived, Paris-based production company, Film Production-Carl Dreyer. The episode marked a period of disillusionment and personal crisis for Dreyer that culminated in his nervous breakdown. Dreyer would not return to filmmaking until the early 1940s with the short film, *Good Mothers* (1942), before working on a film adaptation of the Hans Wiers-Jenssen play, *Anne Pedersdotter*, entitled *Day of Wrath* that explores issues of repression, religious hypocrisy, and fanaticism.

Screen for Reference

The President（《审判长》，1919 年）
Michael（《麦克尔》，1924 年）
Master of the House（《一屋之主》，1925 年）
Gertrud（《葛楚》，1964 年）

New Words

nebulous /'nebjələs/ *adj.*
vague and not clearly defined or not easy to describe 朦胧的，模糊的
finalize /'faɪnəlaɪz/ *v.*
complete 完成，结束，落实
compensate /'kɒmpenseɪt/ *v.*
make up for, make payment to 补偿，弥补

estrangement /ɪ'streɪndʒmənt/ *n.*

being alienated from someone 疏远，不和

expediency /ɪkˈspiːdiənsi/ *n.*

doing what is convenient rather than what is morally right 权宜之计，方便

cerebral /sə'riːbrəl/ *adj.*

relating to the mind rather than the feelings 理智的，智力的

titular /ˈtɪtjulə(r)/ *adj.*

having a particular title or status but no real power or authority 名义上的，有名无实的，徒有虚名的

innate /ɪ'neɪt/ *adj.*

being talented through inherited quality 先天的，与生俱来的

conciliatory /kən'sɪliətɔːri/ *adj.*

having the intention or effect of making angry people calm 调解的

transcendent /træn'sendənt/ *adj.*

going beyond the usual limits; extremely great 卓越的，杰出的，极其伟大的

palpable /'pælpəbl/ *adj.*

obvious or intense and easily noticed 明显的，可感知的

hypocrisy /hɪ'pɑːkrəsi/ *n.*

behaviour in which somebody pretends to have moral standards or opinions that they do not actually have 伪善，虚伪

fanaticism /fəˈnætɪsɪzəm/ *n.*

extreme beliefs or behaviour, especially in connection with religion or politics（尤指宗教、政治上的）狂热，入迷

Phrase and Expression

out of wedlock

of biological parents not married to each other 私生的，婚外的

dispense with

stop using it or get rid of it completely 摒弃

embarked on

to start to do something new or difficult 开始进行

I. Reading Comprehension.

1. How was he affected by his early life?
2. How did Dreyer select actors for *The President*?
3. What did Dreyer's early films reflect?
4. Who was the most representative of Dreyer's feminine ideal?
5. By which film was *Leaves from Satan's Book* inspired?
6. What was author's opinion of *Leaves from Satan's Book*?
7. How did Dreyer achieve his realized mysticism in *The Passion of Joan of Arc*?
8. Which film led to the failure of Dreyer's production company?

II. Fill in the Blanks with the Words Given Below.

Onscreen space is both two-and three-dimensional. Its two-dimensional character is, of course, ( ) from the fact that film images are projected onto a ( ) surface. Thus, every film picture can be viewed like a ( ), with a design on a two-dimensional surface being the substance of what the viewer experiences. Some filmmakers attempt to emphasize the two-dimensional aspect, creating fascinating ( ) on the plane of screen and calling our attention to them.

Most filmmakers set out to create an illusion of ( ). To accomplish this, they place objects and stage action within the frame in ways aimed at giving qualities of ( ) to onscreen space; the illusion can be quite effective. When the camera ( ) through a locale, viewer have feelings much like those they have when they walk through a locale themselves. When the camera is ( ), the film will show objects as being either in front of or behind another object, at a distance from or close to the viewers, or with other such characteristics of everyday perception of space.

Onscreen space can be manipulated in terms of location, distance and direction, ( ), and volume. In fact, many of the most powerful effects in film involve an ( ) between flatness and depth.

a. reality b. derivative c. depth d. flat e. tracks f. dialysis g. painting h. interplay i. compositions j. accommodation k. stationary l. extent

III. Translation.

Section A: Put the followings into Chinese.

1. Rather than casting the studio actors employed by Nordisk, Dreyer followed his own artistic intuition and elected to assemble his own cast of professional and non-professional actors selected for their appropriate face types to the situational and psychological profile of the characters that they portray.

2. The untimely death of his birth mother, Josephine, and the emotional distance of his adoptive mother, Inger Marie, would invariably manifest in Dreyer's highly idealized (and idealistic) characterization of the inexorably virtuous, self-sacrificing, and oppressed woman.

3. Similar in structure and thematic presentation to *Intolerance*, the film chronicles the destructive consequences of temptation on four historical events: the Crucifixion of Jesus Christ, the Spanish Inquisition, the French Revolution, and the Russo-Finnish War.

4. By concentrating on the physical toll of Joan's psychological ordeal, Dreyer translates the unattainable and resolute piety of Joan the saint into the accessible language of compassion for the pain and suffering of Joan the human, achieving a coexistent and symbiotic relationship between the metaphysical and the corporeal that Dreyer defines as realized mysticism.

5. In dispelling Dreyer's reputation as a director of religious films, the strangely atmospheric and ethereal landscape of *Vampyr* (1931) may be viewed not as a radical departure to his spiritual canon, but as a reflection of his propensity for experimentation.

Section B: Put the followings into English.

纵观电影史，圣女贞德的形象曾多次呈现在银幕上。除了《圣女贞德的审判》这部影片之外，另一部具有完全不同艺术气质的卓越电影是由罗伯特·布列松于1962年拍摄的。圣女贞德在战火中的英勇精神及她的外在之美，经常凸显于主流电影、文学和绘画中。

Text B

Still 7-1

Still 7-2

The Passion of Joan of Arc

para 1 *The Passion of Joan of Arc* is based on a actual trial records concerning the fourteenth-century French teenage military heroine. This 1928 black-and-white silent film directed by Danish master Carl Theodor Dreyer (1889–1968) has been identified as a transcendental film by director and film scholar Paul Schrader in his landmark book *Transcendental Style in Film*. By its very nature the film-going experience transports the viewer to another state of consciousness. Some films allow the audience to enter a dream state; others are time machines that carry viewers to another time period or situational space. Entertainment films and blockbusters can relieve the audience of cares and woes, providing an escape until the lights come up.

para 2 The experience of watching a transcendental film presents an opportunity for the viewer to transcend worldly reality and enter a spiritual state. In a transcendental film, the cinematic technique expresses the atmospheric, psychological and emotional live of the characters and the story. The performers become the characters. The camera style, art direction, and editing of the work form a totality that communicates with the conscious, subconscious, and unconscious existence of the viewer.

para 3 To achieve his narrative and thematic goals, Dreyer made many radical stylistic decisions in this silent film. The most controversial, and proven over time to be highly effective, was the extensive use of close-ups. Many of the shots are so tight that they fill the screen with Joan's anguished face, magnifying her myriad reactions of pain and suffering to the evil, misguided injustice forced on her by the priests.

para 4 Many were critical of Dreyer's bold choice in designing the film through the expansive use of this specific shot. They argued that the close-up should be used sparingly to make a dramatic point during a scenc that was covered in myriad shot sizes, in combinations of long and medium shot. This statement ignores the breadth, power, and diversity of what may appear to some as a singular entity. What does blue mean to a painter, the word white to an Eskimo, and sweet, salt, hot, or sour to a master chef? *The passion of Joan of Arc* is a masterpiece of the close-up. The open-minded, open-hearted viewer will observe that each shot is composed for the moment and suddenly reveals blue as a range of colors and hot as spicy, tangy, or smoky, as a burst, an aftertaste, a constant presence, or a recurring series of taste-bud experiences that retreat and endure.

para 5 The conclusion of *The Passion of Joan of Arc* is a powerful representation of religious strife. As Joan burns at the stake, the horrifying yet poetic image are intercut with the English soldiers launching an attack on the townspeople who witness the murder of their future saint. Dreyer was inspired by the work of Eisenstein, and he employs a powerful example of how montage can generate unrelenting action, as destruction of life is everywhere. Eisenstein's philosophy as a Russian was to utilize montage as a celebration of the people and the unity of the masses for good and harm. Dreyer was interested in the individual; as the montage records countless deaths from one mass of people toward another, it is the central image of Joan's earthly form burning to ashes that prevails. The last shot is of the stake. Joan's body is gone—her soul is at the side of God.

I. Context Clues.

Guess the meanings of the following with the help of the context clues.

1. transcendental film ______________________
2. situational space ______________________
3. blockbusters ______________________
4. worldly reality ______________________
5. a range of colors ______________________

II. Questions for Consideration.

1. What stylistic cinematic language caused the controversy in Dreyer's *The Passion of Joan of Arc*?

2. How did Dreyer employ the montage to deal with the film ending?

Unit Eight

Text A

Faith Trilogy

para 1 "The more mature Bergman becomes as a filmmaker, the more caustically and inexorably he focuses on the destructive forces that flow beneath harmonic culture." So writes Swedish film scholar Mikael Timm. This is true of Bergman's thematic and hermeneutic explorations in the 1960s, and equally so of the films' formal developments. In his most radical decade, Bergman increasingly made films that attack modern culture and its various investments from beneath, in dissonant terms, developing a new, much less tonally "centered" cinema in which violent engagements with alterity, doubt and negativity seem to prevail. As a result, this period of Bergman's work tends to either radically repel or attract viewers and critics alike.

para 2 In his 1999 book *Ingmar Bergman: Magician and Prophet*, Marc Gervais sees Bergman's films as a struggle between the "life force", an affirmational humanistic pole, and abstract negativity, a bleak engagement with nihilism and hopelessness. He sees the best films as balancing the two, and while Gervais doesn't really like the apparent trajectory of Bergman's 1960s films, still admires them for their multi-faceted subversions. What became known as the "faith trilogy" — *Through a Glass Darkly* (1961), *Winter Light* (1962) and *The Silence* (1963) — set the tone for these increasingly harsh explorations.

para 3 With the film *Through a Glass Darkly*, the viewer confronts images of a bare world where those who survive are the rational men of a cold modernity, while those who flounder might have been its best hope. In a protean performance as Karin, Harriet Andersson dishes out both emotional warmth and shards of negativity in her sublime but fragmented engagements with others and the world. Her subjective focus is insufficient to consistently master linear demands, and religious belief is a kind of madness taking her away from reality rather than means to a centering affirmation, when her ethereal fantasies turn to revulsion. (Karin's sensuous wait for God in the attic culminates when she sees him as a spider that tries to penetrate her body)

para 4 On the surface, her father (Gunnar Björnstrand) and husband (Max von Sydow) have adapted to a chilly reality with more success. Karin is most at home with her teenage brother Minus who is engulfed in his own identity crisis as he gallivants around the island rocked with doubt, not at home inside himself or his culture.

para 5 Following her breakdown in the attic Karin is penetrated again, by the all-too-real cold fluid of science as her doctor/husband calmly applies a sedating needle, to which she responds with only marginally more displeasure than to the benign and genuine (but to her, meaningless and perfunctory) words of love he offers throughout the film. Meanwhile, outside awaits the giant spider shape of a helicopter in which von Sydow will accompany her to his secular sureties of institutionalized care.

para 6 Framed by the setting sun through a window, for the first time alone (and indoors) together, at the end of *Through a Glass Darkly* Minus asks his father how they can help Karin and receives a "God is love" lecture. Like earlier declarations of love for his family (to whom he gives Stockholm airport trinkets as presents after arriving home from a trip to central Europe), this man's attempt at a didactic humanist faith here seems extremely forced and tenuous. Yet Minus responds positively to this perfunctory communication in the final line of the film, "Papa spoke to me". And in previously admitting the desire to chart his own daughter's schizophrenia so as to provide stimuli for his writing, the father also exhibits (as throughout the film) here a raw, contradictory kind of honesty typical of Bergman's dark renderings of human desire.

para 7 In *Winter Light* the surface freezing of Gunnar Björnstrand's character is just one component of austere images below which the tension of a barely repressed apocalypse is sustained for less than eighty minutes. Shivering a cold sweat of flu and doubt, he plays a priest who suffers "bad faith", and in the face of his anguish struggles to retain belief through ritualized performance. Even when the only person attending the service is his agnostic lover (Ingrid Thulin) who suffers her own—purely secular—kind of abject love.

para 8 Yet somehow Max von Sydow's brief appearance in *Winter Light* seems the epicenter of it all, as a man worried about "the Chinese" with their rumored nuclear weapons. In so much of Bergman's cinema, anxiety has broad social as well as existential resonance, and here it is through fear of global apocalypse (the film was made during the Cuban Missile Crisis). What is most personally and culturally striking is this almost mute man's total incapacity to go along with even a threadbare performance of hope—in ourselves and in this world, both physical and metaphysical. From the first time we see him, he seems on the other side of an important line to the others. Yet they themselves barely sustain their veneer. Von Sydow's terminal condition is reinforced when his priest's council slips from unhelpful insistence (replying "we must live" to Von Sydow's query, "why must we live?") into a self-obsessed monologue betraying his own private horror.

para 9 Rather than philosophical explication, *The Silence*'s almost wordless images generate our experience and reading of a very open film, concluding the loose trilogy in an unexpected way. The complex combination of an uneasy realism with stark formalism makes for clean and complex deep-focus shots matched with an immaculate hyper-diegetic soundscape. So little is literally said here that the formal affect and hermeneutic generativity of Bergman's sound-image compositions are given space to speak louder than ever.

para 10 Through *The Silence*'s aesthetic matrix we sensuously, yet uncomfortably, watch and feel two sisters and a young boy as they have experiences in the hotel of an alien city. When Gunnel Lindblom combs her hair and washes her clothes and body before one of many solo excursions into the world, the tactile and emotional intimacy is both warmly human and erotic, and like cold machine-like fingernails on chalkboard. Meanwhile, during her own body's eruption in the throes of serious illness, the older sister (Ingrid Thulin) articulates her repulsion—"it's all just erectile tissue and bodily secretions"—in a hateful sputtering at the corporeal (and hence for her, meaningless) nature of existence.

para 11 Thulin plays *The Silence*'s only real "believer"—in truth, reason, knowledge, meaning—and is here a decaying figure associated with death. The sheer sensuality of Lindblom's performance might comparatively offer corporeal affirmation, but the very empowerment of this very "alive" woman can seem reactionary in its binarism (the revenge of the body, against Thulin's hegemonic, rancid Cartesianism). It is ultimately the small boy as a nubile, amorphous figure (without any conventional patriarchal model) that provides the real sense of future possibility in the film, as he bears witness to the enactments, investments and dysfunction of his elders.

Screen for Reference

Through a Glass Darkly（《犹在镜中》，1961 年）
Winter Light（《冬日之光》，1963 年）
The Silence（《沉默》，1963 年）
Persona（《假面》，1966 年）

New Words

nihilism /'naɪɪlɪzəm/ *n.*
the belief that nothing has any value, especially that religious and moral principles have no value 虚无主义
trajectory /trə'dʒektəri/ *n.*
the curved path of something that has been fired, hit or thrown into the air（射体在空中的）轨道，弹道，轨迹
shard /ʃɑːrd/ *n.*
a piece of broken glass, metal, etc.（玻璃、金属等的）碎片
sublime /sə'blaɪm/ *adj.*
of very high quality and causing great admiration 庄严的，超群的，令人崇敬的
engulf /ɪn'gʌlf/ *v.*
to surround or to cover somebody/something completely 包围，吞没，淹没
gallivant /'gælɪvænt/ *v.*
to go from place to place enjoying yourself 游玩，游览，闲游
penetrate /'penətreɪt/ *v.*
something to go into or through something 穿过，进入
benign/bɪ'naɪn/ *adj.*

kind and gentle; not hurting anybody 善良的，和善的，慈祥的

didactic /daɪ'dæktɪk/ *adj.*

designed to teach people something, especially a moral lesson 道德说教的，教诲的，教导的

austere /ɔː'stɪə/ *adj.*

simple and plain; without any decorations 朴素的；无装饰的

anguish /'æŋgwɪʃ/ *n.*

severe pain, mental suffering or unhappiness 痛苦，苦恼

repulsion /rɪ'pʌlʃn/ *n.*

a feeling of very strong dislike of something that you find extremely unpleasant 排斥，反感，厌恶

enactment /ɪ'næktmənt/ *n.*

the process of a law becoming official; a law which has been made official 颁布，制订，通过

dysfunction /dɪs'fʌŋkʃn/ *n.*

any disturbance in the function of an organ or body part 功能紊乱

Phrase and Expression

much less

and certainly not 更不用说，何况

dish out

distribute it among a number of people 大量给予或分发

in the throes of

in the middle of an activity, especially a difficult or complicated one 处于……困境（或痛苦）中

I. Reading Comprehension.

1. What did Bergman focus on increasingly while he became more mature as a filmmaker?
2. What's the characteristic of Bergman's work in the early 1960s (such as

the "faith trilogy")?

3. Which three films are known as "faith trilogy"?
4. How do you understand the father's faith?
5. What hided under the surface freezing of Gunnar Björnstrand's character in *Winter Light*?
6. What emotion did much of Bergman's cinema carry in author's view?
7. What was produced by almost wordless images in *The Silence*?
8. What makes for shots matched with soundscape stylistically?

II. Fill in the Blanks with the Words Given Below.

Interpreters and commentators play characters closely ( ) themselves in ( ) and physical appearance, and they interpret these parts dramatically without wholly losing their own ( ). Although they may slightly ( ) themselves to fit the role, they do not attempt to radically change their ( ) personality traits, physical characteristics, or voice qualities. They choose instead to color or interpret the role by filtering it through their own best qualities, ( ) it to fit their own ( ) abilities. The end result is an effective compromise between actor and role, between the real and the assumed identity. The compromise adds a unique creative ( ) to the character being ( ), for in their delivery of the lines these actors ( ) something of their own thoughts and feelings about the character. Thus, these actors may simultaneously comment on and interpret the role. Although the range of roles such actors can play is not as wide as that open to impersonators, it is still relatively broad.

a. inherent b. reveal c. portrayed d. resembling e. assembling f. personality
g. individual h. dimension i. alter j. indigenous k. identity l. modifying

III. Translation.

Section A: Put the followings into Chinese.

1. This period of Bergman's work tends to either radically repel or attract

viewers and critics alike.

2. Marc Gervais sees Bergman's films as a struggle between the "life force", an affirmational humanistic pole, and abstract negativity, a bleak engagement with nihilism and hopelessness.

3. Yet somehow Max von Sydow's brief appearance in *Winter Light* seems the epicenter of it all, as a man worried about "the Chinese" with their rumored nuclear weapons.

4. What is most personally and culturally striking is this almost mute man's total incapacity to go along with even a threadbare performance of hope—in ourselves and in this world, both physical and metaphysical.

5. The complex combination of an uneasy realism with stark formalism makes for clean and complex deep-focus shots matched with an immaculate hyper-diegetic soundscape.

Section B: Put the followings into English.

20 世纪五六十年代是全球电影的黄金时代。这个时期美国观众在电影中寻找意义体验的兴趣，被瑞典电影导演英格玛 · 伯格曼左右着。对那些在好莱坞娱乐圈长大的人来说，英格玛 · 伯格曼的电影是进入艺术电影的大门。包括《野草莓》、《犹在镜中》、《假面》、《处女泉》和《豺狼时刻》在内的大量作品，揭示了关于上帝、死亡和存在的严肃主题，而这些主题是可以用电影来呈现的。

Text B

Still 8-1

Still 8-2

The Seventh Seal

para 1 Bergman did not make films to entertain but to ponder human and spiritual issues. These brooding and liberating works did not fit the paradigm of the Hollywood drama. Bergman's vision of the world was expressed in poetic imagery rich with symbols, signs, and layers of meaning that required an intellectual and emotional commitment from the audience. In return, the films did more than satiate the need to pass time; Bergman's cinema was a central part of a canon that contributed to a new cultural era. Film, the medium of the twentieth century, took its rightful place alongside opera, classical music, and the literate and visual arts. Bergman helped to elevate the movies to an art in which images, text, and sound could deliver an experience that made a lasting and significant impact on the viewer.

para 2 There is little interscene editing in *The Seventh Seal*. Bergman use long takes in which composition and staging bring power and visual dynamics to every frame. In a two-shot the characters often do not look at each other. By allowing the lens to observe both characters as they face in different directions, Bergman examines the strain of intimacy, the physical and psychological relationships they have with each other and with their environment. This approach also gives *The Seventh Seal* a measured pace that alters the viewer's sense of time.

para 3 Sound is very specific. All the voices are post-synched and projected in an up-front perspective into viewer's consciousness. Sound effects are limited but distinctive and used to identify place or mood or to evoke an emotion. There is music, but the overwhelming sound is silence. Viewers are put in touch with their own heart-beating, breathing, and inner thoughts.

para 4 In *The Seventh Seal* there was a significant link among the director's acting company, the troupe portrayed in the film, and the wandering performers who represented the family of Jesus. The actors in the traveling troupe participate in a play within the film, which can also be seen as a film within the film. The troupe is a positive force that tries to uplift a society driven by fear and religious fanaticism. The actors have their own lives and interactions. Jof, Mia, and Mikeal are both symbol of the holy family and flesh-and-blood people struggling with the evil of the plague and the same cardinal questions of purpose as the knight.

para 5 *The Seventh Seal* is an essential film. Woody Alle's career was permanently altered by it, not only in his dramas *Interiors, Another Woman,* and *September*, but in the comedies *Love and Death, A Midsummer Night's Sex Comedy*, and dramedies such as *Hannah and Her Sisters*. American New Wave directors Francis Ford Coppola and Paul Schrader, who came of age in the 1960s and 1970s, were disciples who made the pilgrimage to each and every new Ingmar Bergman film. It is a film that fascinates adolescents who question their own existence. There is a stage when cineastes feel they have outgrown *The Seventh Seal* with its pronouncements concerning death and God. But that passes and we eventually arrive in a place that Ingmar Bergman has never left. It is a place where he plummets into his subconscious, conscious, and personal life for an answer he may only get after the light finally goes out.

I. Context Clues.

Guess the meanings of the following with the help of the context clues.

1. ponder ________________________________
2. paradigm of the Hollywood drama ________________
3. measured pace ____________________________
4. satiate ________________________________
5. pilgrimage ______________________________
6. plummet into ____________________________

II. Questions for Consideration.

1. How do you understand the remark that Bergman did not make films to entertain but to ponder human and spiritual issues?

2. What is the editing trait in *The Seventh Seal*?

Unit Nine

Text A

Storyline and Image in Trilogies of Kaurismäki

para 1 In 1986, Kaurismäki made *Varjoja paratiisissa* (*Shadows in Paradise*), the first film in his "Working-class Trilogy" (aka "Proletariat Trilogy"). With this film, Kaurismäki established the storyline that he would revisit time and time again over the years to follow: the plight of a virtuous, inexpressive outsider who loses everything he has, meets the love of his life, works very hard, and after a series of heartbreaking events, escapes to freedom—which usually lies anywhere outside Finland.

para 2 Nikander, a lonely garbage truck driver (played by Kaurismäki's best friend and favourite leading man, Matti Pellonpää), falls in love with Ilona Rajamäki, a shy supermarket check-out girl (played by Kaurismäki's most frequent leading lady, Kati Outinen). After watching Nikander eat dinner by himself at home, sadly gazing out the window, and then being treated to the equally heartbreaking display of Ilona sitting by herself at a nightclub, the only woman there who is not invited to dance, it is clear that these two belong together.

para 3 From this point forward, *Shadows in Paradise* deconstructs the romantic comedy. When Ilona steals from her corrupt boss in retaliation for unfairly firing her, Nikander helps her out of the resulting jam. The relationship that ensues, however, spirals quickly downward, reaching its climax during Nikander's English-language class, at which the phrase of the day is "It's funny. It's very funny. And it's a lot of fun, too, being in love". These words—which also seem to capture a fragment of Kaurismäki's worldview—inspire Nikander to run out of the school, confront Ilona at her new job and perform his version of the quintessential romantic comedy finale—sweeping the heroine off her feet. "You're coming with me", he announces. "Where?" Ilona asks. "On a honeymoon. You can't make it on your own." That's that, and the couple happily escapes to Estonia. As with the simplicity of the set-up, the efficiency of the resolution is so exaggerated, it's hilarious.

para 4 In the 1990s, Finland began to suffer a severe economic crisis. A major recession hit the northern, industrial part of Finland, leading to several years in which about half a million people were without jobs. Although many of his previous films directly addressed Finland's floundering economy, when the recession struck Kaurismäki became particularly concerned: "If I didn't make a film about unemployment now I wouldn't have the nerve to look at my face in the mirror." The result was 1996's *Kauas pilvet karkaavat* (*Drifting Clouds*), the first film of Kaurismäki's "Loser Trilogy" (aka "Finland Trilogy"), which, along with the "Working-class Trilogy", contains the most representative and important work of his career.

para 5 Like the "Working-class Trilogy", the films in the "Loser Trilogy" were minimalist comedies. But, although a few of Kaurismäki's previous films—most notably *The Match Factory Girl*—were melodramas, *Drifting Clouds* and the two films that followed marked a time of refined focus for Kaurismäki, who was now more invested than ever in showing the economic hardships and social obstacles facing working-class Finns with compassion and even seriousness, in a style indebted to the warm humanism of Frank Capra. And, while the world encountered by his characters was bleaker than ever, the cinematography grew even more luminous in response, taking his trademark saturated colours, velvety shadows and glowing lights to dazzling new heights.

para 6 *Drifting Clouds* follows a husband and wife, Lauri (Kari Väänänen) and Ilona (Kati Outinen), who lose their jobs as tram-driver and head waitress. The economic pressures of unemployment lead to a marital crisis. Although all the cards seemed stacked against the couple, a group effort eventually leads to the successful opening of a new eatery, Restaurant Work, and, indeed, Kaurismäki describes *Drifting Clouds* as a tribute to "the peculiarly Finnish quality that translates roughly as perseverance".

para 7 The film's rich colour design recalls Douglas Sirk's 1950s weepies and helps to fill in the emotional blanks left by the sparse dialogue. For instance, when Lauri and Ilona's new television set is repossessed, the couple is shown in a long-shot, standing completely still as two men remove the television. They say nothing, but the entire living room is emblazoned in a deep royal blue, with a bright scarlet sofa in the centre. Visually, the image throbs. This, and the many other shots like it, are largely a testament to Kaurismäki's outstanding cinematographer, Timo Salminen, who has shot every one of his films. Kaurismäki says that he composes the images but gives Salminen complete control over lighting; this division of labour might help to account for the almost magical tension between the down-to-earth settings and the ethereal cinematography that they are rendered in. The esthetic might vary from one film to another—ranging from the expressionistic chiaroscuro of *Hamlet Goes Business* to the lyrical natural landscapes in moments of *Ariel*, and from the cold industrial scenery of *The Match Factory Girl* to the hallucinatory primary colours of *Drifting Clouds*—but Salminen's remarkable range of styles all create a world in which practical reality is visually amplified in some way.

para 8 Kaurismäki's visual and storytelling abilities reached their apex with 2002's *Mies vailla menneisyyttä (The Man Without a Past*), a love story between two adorably innocent characters set against a grim backdrop of crime and impoverishment. The film, the second in his "Loser Trilogy", was met with worldwide acclaim, winning the Grand Prix at the Cannes Film Festival and earning an Oscar nomination for Best Foreign Language Film.

para 9 A man (Markku Peltola) arrives via train in an anonymous city and is immediately mugged and beaten. He regains consciousness only to find that he has amnesia and so is forced to start his life anew, forging a makeshift home in a container park and falling in love with the Salvation Army worker who helps him get back on his feet. In Kaurismäki's words, "I wanted to make a film about homelessness without making it so socially declaring. The idea of a man without memory, without a past, made it more like a B movie."

para 10 Kaurismäki paints the bureaucratic government as oppressors of the working class through deadpan caricatures that are very funny, but at the same time frighteningly close to reality, suggesting that the inequality of Finnish society borders on the absurd. What kind of society rewards greed instead of work, the film asks, and forces its most ethical members into crime in order to do what is right when the government does wrong?

para 11 A more personal social challenge is confronted by the man's love interest, Irma (Kati Outinen). Irma has a job, but faces another problem shared by many Finns, employed and unemployed alike:

loneliness. In one key scene, Irma changes for bed, neatly hanging her Salvation Army uniform on her otherwise-empty clothes rack, and carefully placing a mat underneath the door crack to shut out the hallway light from the dingy women's dormitory where she lives. Then, something entirely unexpected happens: she slowly turns her head to look almost directly at the camera, if to say to the audience, "This is what happens to the people you always ignore".

para 12 After this jarring moment, there is a sudden shift in tone: Irma looks down at a small tape recorder on her bedside table and hits play. The 1950s rock song *Do the Shake*, which instructs listeners to start dancing wildly, starts to play, and Irma proceeds to solemnly remove and fold her bathrobe. Maintaining her poker face, she casually throws the robe to the side, as though the music has inspired her to become somewhat reckless in her usual bedtime routine. She gets under the covers and looks hopefully toward the alarm clock on her nightstand as the song continues to play. This, as much as any single moment, epitomizes that unique co-existence of comedy and tragedy that is at the heart of Kaurismäki's work.

para 13 As *Do the Shake* continues to play, the film cuts to a shot of the man sitting at the waterfront, then to the Helsinki skyline and then to several shots of homeless people sleeping on the streets, transforming *Do the Shake* into a much broader kind of commentary: connecting Irma to our hero as well as to Finland's homeless population, extending the sympathy we feel toward her to all of the others who come after, and comparing the economic impoverishment of the country to the emotional isolation of one individual.

para 14 Despite all this sorrow, the film ultimately conveys an extraordinary hopefulness based on the fundamental goodness of the working class. In the end, the man survives thanks to others living in the container park community: homeless, jobless men and women whose generosity is thrown into greater relief by the fact that they have nothing of their own. This same hopefulness is expressed in their blossoming relationship between Irma and the man, which develops like a schoolyard romance between two Victorian ten-year-old. After the man walks Irma home one night after work, she thanks him and the man responds by flatly exclaiming, "Look out!" "What?", Irma asks. "There's something in your eye", announces the man, who then slowly leans forward and kisses her lightly on the cheek. Irma lowers her head in shame, and then looks back up at the man: "You stole a kiss." "Forgive me", he says, "I'm not a gentleman". The exchange is hilarious but also remarkably touching—another example of Kaurismäki's ability to delicately balance irony and sentimentality in his magical, self-contained universe.

Screen for Reference

Shadows in Paradise（《天堂孤影》，1986 年）

Ariel（《升空号》，1988 年）

The Match Factory Girl（《火柴厂女工》，1990 年）

Drifting Clouds（《浮云世事》，1996 年）

The Man Without a Past（《没有过去的男人》，2002 年）

Lights in the Dusk（《薄暮之光》，2007 年）

New Words

plight /plaɪt/ *n.*

a difficult and sad situation 困境

virtuous /ˈvɜrtʃuəs/ *adj.*

behaving in a very good and moral way 有道德的，善良的

spiral /'spaɪrəl/ *n.*

a curve that lies on the surface of a cylinder or cone and cuts the element at a constant angle 螺旋（线），旋涡，螺旋形物

quintessential /ˌkwɪntɪ'senʃl/ *adj.*

the perfect example of something, the most important features of something (essence) 精髓的，典型的

hilarious /hɪ'leəriəs/ *adj.*

marked by or causing boisterous merriment or convulsive laughter 欢闹的，非常滑稽的

minimalist /'mɪnɪməlɪst/ *n.*

a practitioner or advocate of artistic minimalism 极简抽象派艺术家

saturate /'sætʃəreɪt/ *v.*

to fill somebody/something completely with something so that it is impossible or useless to add any more 使饱和

velvety /'velvəti/ *adj.*

pleasantly smooth and soft 柔软的

stack /stæk/ *v.*

arranged in a stack 堆积

sparse /spɑːs/ *adj.*

only present in small amounts or numbers and often spread over a large area 稀少的

emblazon /ɪm'bleɪzn/ *v.*

decorate with colors 用纹章装饰，颂扬

throb /θrɒb/ *n.*

a deep pulsating type of pain 跳动，悸动

ethereal /i'θɪəriəl/ *adj.*

characterized by lightness and insubstantiality; as impalpable or intangible as air 天上的，轻飘的

hallucinatory /hə'luːsɪnətri/ *adj.*

partaking of hallucination 幻觉的，引起幻觉的

impoverishment /ɪm'pɒvərɪʃmənt/ *n.*

the state of having little or no money and few or no material possessions 贫穷

makeshift /'meɪkʃɪft/ *adj.*

used temporarily for a particular purpose because the real thing is not available 临时的，凑合的，权宜之计的

deadpan /'dedpæn/ *adj.*

without any expression or emotion; often pretending to be serious when you are joking 没有表情的

reckless/'rekləs/ *adj.*

characterized by careless unconcerned 鲁莽的，不顾危险的

epitomize /ɪ'pɪtəmaɪz/ *v.*

to be a perfect example of something 成为……的缩影，集中体现

Phrase and Expression

fill in

to do somebody's job for a short time while they are not there 填补，代替

account for

to be the explanation or cause of something 说明，导致

I. Reading Comprehension.

1. What's the classic storyline of Kaurismäki's films?
2. How is the romantic dealt with in *Shadows in Paradise*?
3. What's the background of *Drifting Clouds*?
4. What is the response of Kaurismäki to the people being laid off work in the economic crisis of Finland in 1990s?
5. What is the narrative style in the films of the "Working-class Trilogy" and the "Loser Trilogy"?
6. How does the color in *Drifting Clouds* affect the emotion of the viewers?

7. What does the picture in *The Man Without a Past* convey as film cuts to a shot of the sitting man at the waterfront, then to skyline and then to some other images with the song *Do the Shake* going on?
8. How does Kaurismäki show his ability to balance irony and sentimentality in this film?

II. Fill in the Blanks with the Words Given Below.

Time in a film-conveyed by the order and pace with which images, events, and actions succeed one another—is of three kinds: dramatic time, physical time, and affective time. Dramatic time is structured by the demands of ( ), characterization, ( ), and other features of story development. Events of very large ( ), such as the Napoleonic War against Russia, can be ( ) via dramatic time in no more than a few hours—as in the several versions of *War and Peace*. Typically, when an event is represented in terms of dramatic time, much is ( ). A viewer need not see all ( ) of an action in order to identify it or for it to form part of an aesthetically satisfying whole.

Very few films are structured ( ) according to physical time. *Cleo from 5 to 7* is a notable example of one that is. Physical time, then, refers to a filmic structuring of events at the same ( ) at which they would occur in the world ( ) movie.

In affective time, events are ordered so as to have certain affects upon the audience's ( ) sense of time. Thus, some scenes—depending on the order and pace of events—will be made to seem slow moving, other to fly by.

a. phases b. plot c. subjective d. theme e. omitted f. outside g. rate h. outworn i. scope j. scroll k. portrayed l. entirely

III. Translation.

Section A: Put the followings into Chinese.

1. With this film, Kaurismäki established the storyline that he would

revisit time and time again over the years to follow: the plight of a virtuous, inexpressive outsider who loses everything he has, meets the love of his life, works very hard, and after a series of heartbreaking events, escapes to freedom—which usually lies anywhere outside Finland.

2. Although many of his previous films directly addressed Finland's floundering economy, when the recession struck Kaurismäki became particularly concerned: "If I didn't make a film about unemployment now I wouldn't have the nerve to look at my face in the mirror."

3. *Drifting Clouds* and the two films that followed marked a time of refined focus for Kaurismäki, who was now more invested than ever in showing the economic hardships and social obstacles facing working-class Finns with compassion and even seriousness.

4. The esthetic might vary from one film to another—ranging from the expressionistic chiaroscuro of *Hamlet Goes Business* to the lyrical natural landscapes in moments of *Ariel*, and from the cold industrial scenery of *The Match Factory Girl* to the hallucinatory primary colours of *Drifting Clouds*—but Salminen's remarkable range of styles all create a world in which practical reality is visually amplified in some way.

5. What kind of society rewards greed instead of work, the film asks, and forces its most ethical members into crime in order to do what is right when the government does wrong?

Section B: Put the followings into English.

在艺术中，语境意味着一切。《雌雄大盗》是基于 20 世纪 30 年代克莱德·巴罗与邦尼·帕克这对银行劫匪的真实故事改编的。编剧罗伯特·本顿、大卫·纽曼，明星制片人沃伦·比蒂及导演阿瑟·佩恩的拍摄目的是拍摄一部能反映 1967 年美国人生活的电影，而不是大萧条时期的黑帮片。

Text B

Still 9-1

Still 9-2

Bonnie and Clyde

para 1 In retrospect, *Bonnie and Clyde* marks a turning point in American filmmaking. Throughout the 1960s the studio system was collapsing. Warner Brothers, the studio best known for its gangster cycle in the 1930s and 1940s featuring James Cagney, Humphrey Bogart, and Edward G. Robinson, was in the process of being sold off when it distributed *Bonnie and Clyde*. Mogul Jack Warner, distracted by the coming end of his reign, left the film in the hands of producer Warren Beatty and director Arthur Penn.

para 2 Bonnie and Clyde are antiestablishment figures. They despise the government, the financial establishment, and law enforcement—the military—industrial complex of their time. Like hippies and many young people of the 1960s, Bonnie and Clyde were rebels. They rebelled against all bureaucracies. Bonnie and Clyde only trusted people of their own age. Elders in power, like Sheriff Frank Hamer (Denver Pyle), were to be defied, ridiculed, and brought down by a revolution that returned power to the people. The banks were rich, the people were poor. Peace was not the way. Only violent action could change the world. After the revolution they could live their lives, but first Bonnie and Clyde had to destroy everything that was wicked.

para 3 Thematically, *Bonnie and Clyde* created a new paradigm for the American film. Stylistically, it broke away from traditional Hollywood conventions by creating a visual style that would lead to a new aesthetic model for young filmmakers.

para 4 *Bonnie and Clyde* is a road movie. They steal cars to move around the country and keep ahead of the law. Many scenes take place in cars, dealing with dreams, aspirations, and the reality Bonnie and Clyde find themselves in. When the heat is on and they are running out of supplies, they stop at a roadside community of displaced people. This little tent village is made up of homeless Americans living on the barest of necessities. When Clyde drives up and asks for help, they feed the gang and encircle the car to gaze at the legends in person. In 1967 young people were living on communes all over the United States. If Jimi Hendrix, Jim Morrison, or Janis Joplin had stopped off at a commune for some brown rice, Wine, apple juice, or a toke off a joint, this is what it would have looked Like.

para 5 Instead of a dramatic underscore, *Bonnie and Clyde* features the authentic bluegrass guitar and banjo music of Lester Flatt and Earl Scruggs. Their *Foggy Mountain Breakdown* captured time and place while also sonically supporting the manic energy of the rebellious couple in action.

para 6 *Bonnie and Clyde* established that the American film could reflect the lives of the audience regardless of genre, period, story, or the genesis of the characters. It was a violent film for violent times, graphically portraying both the physical and emotional results of the current milieu. Arthur Penn directed a film that started a revolution. Inspired by the history of film and theater and plugged into the zeitgeist, Penn, Warren Beatty, and the entire cast and crew of *Bonnie and Clyde* rewrote the Hollywood playbook. America was never the same after the sixties. American film stepped up to the challenges presented by a new generation—the medium has not been the same since.

I. Context Clues.

Guess the meanings of the following with the help of the context clues.

1. in retrospect ______________________________
2. antiestablishment figures ______________________
3. paradigm ______________________________
4. gangster cycle ____________________________
5. current milieu ____________________________

II. Questions for Consideration.

1. By author's opinion *Bonnie and Clyde* reflects the lives of the audience, do you agree? Why?

2. Why does the author say Arthur Penn directed a film that started a revolution?

Unit Ten

Text A

Lars von Trier

para 1 In the last 20 years, Lars von Trier has created such works as the so-called "Europe Trilogy", which embraces his first three feature films, *The Element of Crime* (1984), *Epidemic* (1987), and *Europa* (1991) — impressive, though also somewhat cold and artificial, comments on critical times in Europe of the future, present and past. In 1994, Lars von Trier marked a new phase with *The Kingdom*, a TV series blending horror with humour, which became his big popular breakthrough and radically changed his relationship to cinematic language and technique. An international breakthrough followed with *Breaking the Waves* (1996) and the Cannes Palme d'Or winner *Dancer in the Dark* (2000), *Dogville* (2003) and *Manderlay* (2005) have exhibited a new and challenging blend of tradition and innovation.

para 2 Most radically, he has challenged the film establishment, and himself, with the Dogme concept, a fertile wave washing over Danish cinema as both effective international branding and a shortcut to artistic reinvention. His own contribution to the Dogme oeuvre, *The Idiots* (1998), may well be his most original work.

para 3 Lars von Trier's production is an odd combination of extreme consistency and constant experimentation and dynamic change. There is continual innovation and stylistic change, yet every project is an experiment pointing in the same direction. He once said, " Perhaps that's what auteurism is to me: it's about heading in the direction you are called. it's still an exploration, though that's such an overused term. I wouldn't say that I'm going further out into the extremes of film. I just take a few old principles and try to have fun with them, like a carpenter exploring the different potentials of wood". Lars von Trier can rightfully be said to echo Picasso's statement: "I don't search, I find."

para 4 Lars von Trier's public image is a combination of detached, complex artist and challenging media personality. You might say, oxymoronically, that he is a shy exhibitionist. Likewise, as an artist, he likes to operate in the intersection between two opposing tendencies. He is an avant-gardist, an advance scout into the territory of new possibilities, which would usually mean moving in the narrow circles of experimental film. Lars von Trier, however, has managed to address a large and growing international mainstream audience. As he points out, control and loss of control are opposite poles of his artistic process. His early films show an almost manic need for control. The cinematic expression, the technique, the dramatic construction, everything is marked by a refined perfectionism. Everything is calculated and planned, everything is willed. There is something puppet-like about Europa: the characters seem like marionettes in a complex technical frame.

para 5 Lars von Trier calls it a "pathological need for perfectionism" that "in part, has kept me from producing technically predefined images in my films for years now, which in practice means no planned camera setups". *The Kingdom* was the turning point at which he deliberately abandoned control (although one could reasonable claim that a self-chosen loss of control is still under your control). Dictated by outside conditions—a long script which could not be realized in the normal way within the time frame available to *The Kingdom*—he decided to abandon his usual time-consuming professional care and instead leave such delaying factors as lighting, point of view, composition and picture quality to chance. As the success of *The Kingdom* proved, the degree of finish we are used to in professional productions is not so important, really, it may even be outright insignificant, as long as the story and the characters hold sufficient interest. Based on that experience, Lars von Trier developed the Dogme 95 manifesto (written in early 1995, shortly after *The Kingdom* was broadcast). Lars von Trier had always liked working according to self-imposed rules. In Dogme 95, assisted by Thomas Vinterberg, he formulated a system of rules for the kind of obstacle course he finds stimulating to the artistic process. The Dogme manifesto's Vow of Chastity—10 commandments specifying mainly what the director may not do—is a challenge to the filmmaker intended to force him away from habit and convention. Just as it would be a challenge, perhaps even an inspiration, for an Italian chef to have to cook without pasta, olive oil, tomatoes, oregano, parmesan cheese, etc., it is a challenge for the filmmaker to be denied his ingrained routines and inclinations. There is more than a touch of masochism in this approach to art making. This self-torture should be seen as a way to force mold-breaking results. The Dogme artist punishes himself in the ways that hurt the most, in the expectation that it will lead to artistic liberation. While most stick to convention and work within the established norms, Lars von Trier forces himself to try out new ways of doing things. As early as *Epidemic*, he proclaimed, "a film should be like a pebble in your shoe". In a manner of speaking, Dogme is institutionalized masochistic renunciation as a designated path to artistic development, asceticism as a path to blossoming. He has carried this over into his recent works, which are not Dogme films but follow other complex, inhibiting rules. Moreover, Lars von Trier recently announced that he has drawn up a special set of rules for three Danish-Scottish features, a project known as The Advance Party. In *The Five Obstructions* (2003, co-directed by Jørgen Leth), Lars von Trier expands his masochistic approach into a kind of sadism. Since his painful method produces results in his own work, it seems logical to assume that it would work for others, as well. The idea of having Leth reshoot *The Perfect Human* five times according to principles devised by Lars von Trier is fun, of course—Lars von Trier always is—but there is a kind of seriousness, too—again, with Lars von Trier, there always is. The obstructions set up for Leth, based on the principle that anything Leth would prefer to do, he cannot, is an excellent joke, but the method actually produces results for Leth, and Lars von Trier.

para 6 The issue of control or loss of control is concretely reflected in how you use the camera. As Lars von Trier has discussed, there are two essentially different things you can do with a camera: framing and pointing. You can strive for perfectionism in carefully planned and controlled shots unfolding within the precisely calculated frame of the camera. Or you can go out into the here and now and see what happens when you impulsively point the camera at an event that seems exciting and relevant. The framing method, with its complete control, fosters formalism, while the pointing method, with its loss of control, fosters realism—the polished versus the raw.

para 7 In his early films, Lars von Trier practiced framing to the nth degree. *The Kingdom* was an experiment with the pointing method that became dominant in Dogme and later works, where a partly improvised camera style does not have to adhere to any of a number of visual and aesthetic requirements, but simply and functionally follows the actor.

While Lars von Trier in his early films had a detached relationship to his actors and clearly wanted to keep his distance, his new method, which really begins with *Breaking the Waves*, takes him close in. Lars von Trier was the main cameraman on *The Idiots*, *Dancer in the Dark*, *Dogville* and *Manderlay*, which enabled the closest possible contact with the actors during individual takes.

para 8 Lars von Trier's films, with all their striking formal, stylistic and technical features, also strike up big themes. The early films—*Pictures of Liberation*, the Europa trilogy and up to and including *The Kingdom*—show an explicit intoxication with demonic dystopia, featuring an idealist character drawn down into the darkness. The films that follow are about women sacrificing themselves. *Breaking the Waves* startlingly links religion to erotic and masochistic elements. Martyrdom is a theme that continues into *Dancer in the Dark*, with music as redemption. *Dogville*, too, is marked by the female sense of the victim role—then, suddenly, the theme ends. Enough is enough. While "kill your darlings" could be a motto for Lars von Trier's style and method, it is also the specific plan of action for the female protagonist in *Dogville.*

para 9 Socio-political themes are struck in *Dancer in the Dark*, *Dogville* and the recently released *Dear Wendy*, directed by Thomas Vinterberg from Lars von Trier screenplay. The two films formulate a critique of America that continues into his own latest directorial effort, *Manderlay,* as the character of Grace from *Dogville* continues exploring American society, now on a southern plantation that still practices slavery.

para 10 With enormous vitality, Lars von Trier has evolved from an eccentric avant-gardist into a humanized, still challenging artist and a major entrepreneur, via the Zentropa production company and the Filmbyen studios in Avedøre near Copenhagen, and a source of inspiration to his Dogme brothers and sisters. His stature in Danish cinema, where his importance continues to take new twists and turns, is matched by his international stature as one of the most relevant filmmakers working today.

Screen for Reference

The Element of Crime（《犯罪元素》，1984 年）
The Kingdom（《医院风云》，1994 年）
Breaking the Waves（《破浪》，1996 年）
Dancer in the Dark（《黑暗中的舞者》，2000 年）

New Words

embrace /ɪm'breɪs/ *v.*
to accept an idea, a proposal, a set of beliefs, etc., especially when it is done with enthusiasm 拥抱，信奉，皈依，包含
fertile /'fɜːtaɪl/ *adj.*
capable of reproducing 肥沃的，能生育的
oeuvre /'ɜːvrə/ *n.*
the total output of a writer or artist 全部作品
manic /'mænɪk/*adj.*
affected with or marked by frenzy or mania uncontrolled by reason 躁狂的，患躁狂病的
marionette /ˌmæriə'net/ *n.*
a puppet whose different parts you can move using strings or wires 牵线木偶
formulate /'fɔːrmjuleɪt/ *v.*
come up with(an idea, plan, explanation, theory, or principle) after a mental effort, express it or describe it using particular words 构想，表达

inclination /ˌɪnklɪ'neɪʃn/ *n.*

a feeling that makes you want to do something, a tendency to do something 倾向

masochistic /ˌmæsə'kɪstɪk/ *adj.*

deriving pleasure or sexual gratification from being abused or dominated 受虐狂的，自讨苦吃的

renunciation /rɪˌnʌnsi'eɪʃn/ *n.*

rejecting or disowning or disclaiming as invalid 声明放弃（权利等），宣布断绝关系

asceticism /ə'setɪsɪzəm/ *n.*

rigorous self-denial and active self-restraint 禁欲主义，苦行主义

concretely /'kɒŋkri:tli/ *adv.*

in concrete terms 具体地

improvise /'ɪmprəvaɪz/ *v*

perform without preparation 即兴创作；临时提供，临时凑成

intoxication /ɪnˌtɒksɪ'keɪʃn/ *n.*

a temporary state resulting from excessive consumption of alcohol 陶醉

redemption /rɪ'dempʃn/ *n.*

the act of purchasing back something previously sold 赎回，偿还，补救

motto /'mɒtəʊ/ *n.*

a favorite saying of a sect or political group 座右铭，格言

vitality /vaɪ'tæləti/ *n.*

energy and enthusiasm 活力，生命力

eccentric /ɪk'sentrɪk/ *adj.*

considered by other people to be strange or unusual 古怪的，反常的

Phrase and Expression

in a manner of

in a particular way, in a way 凭借……方式

to the nth degree

extremely; to an extreme degree 极其

I. Reading Comprehension.

1. What does Danish cinema derive from Dogma concept?

2. How does Lars von Trier describe the auteurism?

3. Why do Dogme artists make up rules to restrict themselves?

4. Can you give a description of Lars von Trier's public image and his personality?

5. What did he deliberately do when producing the TV series *The Kingdom*?

6. What is the universal recognition of *The Kingdom* in his creation?

7. What's the difference between Lars von Trier's early and later works in main themes and frame style?

8. What are the two methods to handle a camera according to Lars von Trier? What's the difference?

II. Fill in the Blanks with the Words Given Below.

A political economy of cinema is therefore necessary if we are to understand why and how certain types of films get produced and distributed; the industrial ( ) and practices that structure the form and content of these film ( ); and how audiences select and ( ) them. It offers a way of understanding the power relations involved in film ( ) and ( ), and contributes towards a more historical analysis of cinema. Many critics, including Marxists, criticize this form of analysis, and claim that it presents cultural forms as a simple ( ) of economic activities and interests. However, economic determinism is not a ( ) consequence of taking industrial and economic practices into account. Rather, political economy allows an analysis of the ways in which the relations of cultural production affect the formal properties of texts. Too often theorists anxious to avoid economic determinism have thrown the baby out with the bath-water, and ( ) the autonomy of cultural forms. Furthermore, critics who ( ) political economy and focus on the ( ) properties of film texts still tend to assume that these texts reflect dominant economic interests.

a. automatic b. ideological c. processes d. interpret e. consumption f. reflection g. dismiss h. overemphasized i. production j. mainstream k. texts l. processes

III. Translation.

Section A: Put the followings into Chinese.

1. There is continual innovation and stylistic change, yet every project is an experiment pointing in the same direction.

2. He is an avant-gardist, an advance scout into the territory of new possibilities, which would usually mean moving in the narrow circles of experimental film.

3. As the success of *The Kingdom* proved, the degree of finish we are used to in professional productions is not so important, really, it may even be outright insignificant, as long as the story and the characters hold sufficient interest.

4. The Dogme manifesto's Vow of Chastity—10 commandments specifying mainly what the director may not do—is a challenge to the filmmaker intended to force him away from habit and convention.

5. *The Kingdom* was an experiment with the pointing method that became dominant in Dogme and later works, where a partly improvised camera style does not have to adhere to any of a number of visual and aesthetic requirements, but simply and functionally follows the actor.

Section B: Put the followings into English.

什么造就了法国电影新浪潮？那时，法国电影的发展是停滞的。曾经的大师或去世，或退休，或始终一成不变地重复着自己。这时出现了一批新生代的电影人，他们有着不同的背景，这有异于他们的前辈。作为一个评论家，弗朗索瓦·特吕弗理解那些伟大的导演，如阿尔弗莱德·希区柯克、霍华德·霍克斯及约翰·福特，是如何用影像来诠释主题的。他的那些法国同行创新性的评论及电影作品激发了一种冒险精神，创造了一种氛围，促使他们以个人的作品为出发点，逐渐形成了一个运动。

Text B

Still 10-1

Still 10-2

Jules and Jim

para 1 The principal narrative of *Jules and Jim* is a simple one from which emerge complex characters and intricate consequences for all. Jules (Oskar Werner) and Jim (Henri Serre) both fall in love with Catherine (Jeanne Moreau), a woman with a mercurial personality filled with passionate motivations and a swirling disposition totally dedicated to her needs and desires. *Jules and Jim* is not just a ménage à trois; the relationship among the three is an investigation into the nature of love, sex, respect, individual freedom, the bond between two and three people, and the strength and fragility of connections.

para 2 *Jules and Jim* is photographed in a widescreen format that references black-and-white Cinemascope films of the 1950s. This aspect ratio is also effective in presenting the three characters in a single locked-off or moving shot while anchoring them in their environment. This especially applies to vital scenes in the countryside, where they are free to explore their social experiment.

para 3 The fluidity and pace of *Jules and Jim* is linked more to American than French cinema, But Truffaut departs from Hollywood by relying on a handheld and moving camera and the rhythm of action and dialogue rather than montage. The editing punctuates moods and emotional states with jump cuts, or a series of angels cut together to express the inner life of the characters. These moments do not interfere with the overall languid pace of *Jules and Jim* that establishes the movement of life in an earlier time. Editing accentuates Catherine's independent spirit and the way Jules and Jim react to her.

para 4 The French New Wave was a bridge between the classical cinemas of France and the United States—the evolution of the medium that progressed throughout the 1960s, resulting in a new generation of filmmakers who flowered in the 1970s. With *Jules and Jim*, Francois Truffaut challenged the morality portrayed in traditional cinema and liberated the camera from the restrictions of the tripod and studio lights. However, the dissolve, the classical article of grammar where one image fades in while another fades out to suggest the passage of time, is used throughout the film.

para 5 The lessons and achievements of *Jules and Jim* and the French New Wave are lasting. Truffaut and his colleagues invigorated the cinema with a resonance that reflected the vibrant era in which they lived and created a new aesthetic paradigm that paid homage to the past while opening new vistas for future generation of filmmakers.

I. Context Clues.

Guess the meanings of the following with the help of the context clues.

1. mercurial personality ______________________
2. swirling ______________________

3. locked-off camera ______________________________

4. fragility ______________________________

5. punctuate ______________________________

6. paid homage to the past ______________________________

II. Questions for Consideration.

1. *Jules and Jim*, according to the author, is not just a ménage à trois. Do you agree with it? Why?

2. How does editing function in *Jules and Jim*?

后　记

在经过多年的思考和课堂试用后，我萌生了把这些经过检验的材料编写成书，以供更多的人阅读和使用的想法。以原文的形式加一些辅助性的思考练习，将其编写成一本教材，这既是学习语言的工具，更是电影专业的学生接触电影专业原著，直接了解作者观点、影片导演创作手段和创作风格的最佳窗口。在进行了广泛深入的调研和论证，精心的资料搜集和课文内容设计后，我和我的团队终于完成了《电影经典文本导读》教材的编写工作。在成稿之前，我们已对试用中出现的问题和不足做了修改和调整。期望这本书在使学生丰富电影专业知识、提升审美趣味的同时，也能激发他们在创作过程中的灵感。

感谢所有支持我们编写工作的老师和同学们！

编者

2020 年 11 月 27 日

图书在版编目（CIP）数据

电影经典文本导读 / 宋雁蓉主编. —北京：中国国际广播出版社，2021.5（2023.9重印）

ISBN 978-7-5078-4907-3

Ⅰ.①电… Ⅱ.①宋… Ⅲ.①英语－阅读教学－高等学校－教材②电影文学剧本－世界 Ⅳ.①H319.37

中国版本图书馆CIP数据核字（2021）第098243号

电影经典文本导读

主　　编	宋雁蓉
副 主 编	施嘉敏　朱　琳
责任编辑	张晓梅
校　　对	张　娜
版式设计	邢秀娟
封面设计	赵冰波

出版发行	中国国际广播出版社有限公司［010-89508207（传真）］
社　　址	北京市丰台区榴乡路88号石榴中心2号楼1701 邮编：100079
印　　刷	北京捷迅佳彩印刷有限公司

开　　本	710×1000　1/16
字　　数	180千字
印　　张	8.75
版　　次	2022 年 3 月　北京第一版
印　　次	2023 年 9 月　第三次印刷
定　　价	38.00 元